D1306653

# PRAXIS II®
# POWER PRACTICE
# ELEMENTARY
# EDUCATION

# PRAXIS II®
# POWER PRACTICE
## ELEMENTARY
## EDUCATION:

## CURRICULUM, INSTRUCTION, AND ASSESSMENT
## (0011/5011)

NEW YORK

Cataloging-in-Publication Data is on file with the Library of Congress.

Printed in the United States of America

9 8 7 6 5 4 3 2 1

ISBN 978-1-57685-979-7

For more information on LearningExpress, other LearningExpress products, or bulk sales,
please write to us at:
     80 Broad Street
     4th Floor
     New York, NY 10004

Or visit us at:
     www.learningexpressllc.com

# CONTENTS

# PRAXIS II®
# POWER PRACTICE
# ELEMENTARY
# EDUCATION

CHAPTER

# 1 ▶ INTRODUCTION TO THE PRAXIS II® ELEMENTARY EDUCATION: CURRICULUM, INSTRUCTION, AND ASSESSMENT (0011/5011) TEST

**B**eing a teacher is one of the most important and rewarding jobs a person can choose. However, the journey to finding success in the classroom has many stops along the way. While private schools and religious institutions can set their own requirements for hiring teachers, public schools must follow their state's guidelines for teacher qualifications.

The requirements for working at one of the nearly 100,000 public elementary and secondary schools in the United States are set by the individual states. Most states require that their elementary school teachers achieve both of the following objectives:

- earn a bachelor's or master's degree in education
- pass a state test or Praxis® exam

A state's teacher certification requirements may change frequently. Your state's department of education website should lay out the specific and current requirements to become a teacher where you live. You can also visit the Praxis® website directly to determine the testing requirements based on your state, at www.ets.org/praxis/prxstate.html.

Some states in need of teachers have allowed for certain candidates to become accredited through alternative—and much quicker—routes. Even those applicants, however, will likely need to pass a standardized test. The purpose of this book is to prepare you for that test and get you one step closer to becoming a full-time teacher.

## Praxis® Background

The standardized tests used to determine whether teachers have the core knowledge necessary to do their jobs are mostly developed by a company called the Educational Testing Service (ETS). This is the same company that creates the SAT Reasoning Test™ and many other assessments, such as the Test of English as a Foreign Language (TOEFL™) and the Graduate Record Examination (GRE™).

ETS's series of Praxis® assessments are designed to be used in the teacher certification process. According to ETS's website, the Praxis® tests "measure general and subject-specific knowledge and teaching skills." There are more than 100 different Praxis® tests, ranging from agriculture to world and U.S. history.

## About the Praxis II® Elementary Education: Curriculum, Instruction, and Assessment Test

The Elementary Education: Curriculum, Instruction, and Assessment test is designed for prospective teachers of students in the elementary grades. Those taking the test typically have completed a bachelor's degree program in elementary/middle school education or have prepared through some alternative certification program.

The test, which features 110 total questions to be answered in two hours, covers the range of material a new teacher needs to know to be successful in the classroom. The questions assess both theoretical and practical knowledge. Some of the questions assess how well you are able to plan a curriculum, design instruction, and assess student learning; many pose problems that teachers often must deal with in the classroom; and many are based on real-life examples of student work. Some questions address general issues; however, most are set in the context of subjects most commonly taught in elementary school: reading and language arts, mathematics, science, social studies, the arts, and physical education.

# Overview of the Test

## *Praxis II® Elementary Education: Curriculum, Instruction, and Assessment by the Numbers*

**Total Questions:** 110 Multiple-Choice

**Total Time:** 2 hours

| | TOPICS | |
| --- | --- | --- |
| SUBJECT | NUMBER OF QUESTIONS | PERCENTAGE OF TEST |
| Reading and Language Arts Curriculum, Instruction, and Assessment | 38 | 35% |
| Mathematics Curriculum, Instruction, and Assessment | 22 | 20% |
| Science Curriculum, Instruction, and Assessment | 11 | 10% |
| Social Studies Curriculum, Instruction, and Assessment | 11 | 10% |
| Arts and Physical Education Curriculum, Instruction, and Assessment | 11 | 10% |
| General Information about Curriculum, Instruction, and Assessment | 17 | 15% |

Questions that test **curriculum** knowledge ask about the specific components of each subject area tested and the tools used to teach them. You will need to know how to integrate required concepts for each subject area into a curriculum plan and the equipment, materials, demonstrations, and activities by which topics can be taught.

Questions that test **instruction** knowledge will ask about different teaching methods and their applications in the classroom. Each specific subject test will feature questions asking about best practices for identifying students' knowledge and experience levels and designing a plan to best teach to a group comprised of students with varying aptitudes and motivation levels.

Questions that test **assessment** topics ask about the best ways to evaluate knowledge levels of a stu-

dent group—which methods work for each subject and how to best apply them. Then, questions will also ask about interpreting data observed from testing and classroom observations. Finally, assessment questions test how well prospective teachers identify error patterns in student responses, and common inaccuracies and misconceptions for each subject.

## *Test Subjects*
### Reading and Language Arts Curriculum, Instruction, and Assessment

This section accounts for the largest number of questions on the exam. The 38 questions in this test section cover the curriculum, instruction, and assessment of reading, writing, speaking, listening, and viewing. Prospective elementary grade teachers will need to be well-versed in the design, construction, and implementation of curriculum, and the assessment of student output in topics including phonetic awareness, phonics, language fluency, vocabulary, reading comprehension, types and traits of writing, types of text and structure of text, stages of writing development, writing and evaluating writing using technology, theories of language acquisition, analyzing students' writing, rubrics, and more.

## Mathematics Curriculum, Instruction, and Assessment

This section, comprised of 22 questions, covers the curriculum, instruction, and assessment of elementary-grade math topics, including number operations, pre-algebra and algebra, geometry and measurement, and probability, statistics, and data analysis concepts.

Questions in this section will test your knowledge of mathematics teaching methods; curriculum design of developmentally appropriate problems; use of materials, equipment, texts, and technology; and awareness of the personal, social, and emotional development of students. You will also be expected to know how to teach mathematics to a classroom comprised of various skill levels and types of experience.

Your mathematics assessment knowledge should cover both informal methods (observation and group and peer assessment) and formal methods (quizzes and tests).

## Science Curriculum, Instruction, and Assessment

The science portion of the exam is comprised of 11 questions. This section covers the curriculum, instruction, and assessment of life science, Earth and space science, physical science, and health concepts. Within these subsections of science, you will be expected to know methods for involving the following in teaching methods: science concepts and processes; scientific inquiry; scientific data; model building and forecasting; use of materials, equipment,

texts, and technology; and more. You will need to know how to design a curriculum that meets the needs of a diverse student group.

Your science assessment knowledge should cover both informal methods (group and peer assessment and project learning) and formal methods (quizzes and tests).

## Social Studies Curriculum, Instruction, and Assessment

The social studies portion of the exam is comprised of 11 questions. This section covers the curriculum, instruction, and assessment of geography and history; government, civics, and economics; anthropology and sociology; and historical analysis and interpretation. You will be expected to know instructional methods for meeting a diverse group of students' needs through strategies like projects, guided discovery, and games, and methods for using equipment, texts, and technology like maps, pictures, real-world resources, and the Internet.

Your social studies assessment knowledge should cover both informal methods (teacher observation, interviews, and model building) and formal methods (quizzes and tests).

## Arts and Physical Education Curriculum, Instruction, and Assessment

This section, comprised of 11 questions, covers curriculum, instruction, and assessment of art (including design, art history, and technique), music, and physical education (including exercise, game and sport skills, and health topics).

To succeed on this test section, you will be expected to know various methods of teaching, using a variety of materials, equipment, texts, and technology, that aim to meet a diverse group of students' needs and aptitudes. You will need to know how to properly analyze and score student work in a way that leads to improvement and enrichment.

### General Information about Curriculum, Instruction, and Assessment

The general information section of the exam, comprised of 17 questions, covers teaching strategies and activities that aid in curriculum, instruction, and assessment. You must have a good knowledge of state and national standards for elementary grades, developmentally appropriate curriculum planning, methods for turning standards into age- and grade-appropriate activities and assessments, learning theories and instructional strategies, instructional approaches to classroom management, student motivation strategies, and more. You will also be asked questions on the use of standardized assessments, theories on the basic principles of assessment, and correct and appropriate methods for collaborating with colleagues and community and interacting with parents.

## Paper Delivered versus Computer Delivered

You can take the Praxis II® Elementary Education: Curriculum, Instruction, and Assessment test either as a pencil-and-paper test (0011) or as a computerized test (5011).

The computer-based test is offered year-round, on an ongoing basis. However, if you feel more comfortable taking the exam via hard copy, you can check ETS's Praxis® site at www.ets.org/praxis for test dates (there are usually four pencil-and-paper tests given per year).

### *The Computer-Delivered Test*

The Praxis II® Elementary Education: Curriculum, Instruction, and Assessment test is available as a computer-delivered test in more than 300 locations throughout the United States. Since it is given on an ongoing basis, as soon as you are ready to take the exam, you can register (see later in this chapter for registration information). You don't have to know

much about computers to take the computer-based version—each test begins with a tutorial on the use of the computer. You are encouraged to spend as much time as needed on the tutorial.

All questions for this Praxis test are in multiple-choice format. The questions are presented on the computer screen, and you choose your answers by clicking in the oval next to the correct choice or choices (for multiple-answer math questions).

The computer-based tests now have a special "mark" function, which allows you to "mark" a question that you would like to skip temporarily and come back to at a later time during the same section on the test. Test takers will have a review screen to see whether a question has been answered, not seen yet, or "marked."

The computer-based test is designed to ensure fairness, because each test taker receives the following:

- the same distribution of content
- the same amount of testing time
- the same test directions
- the same tutorials on computer use

### REMINDER

You may take the computer-based test only once a month, and no more than six times over the course of a year. This even applies to situations where you may have canceled your scores. If you violate this rule, your retest scores will not be reported, and your fees will not be refunded.

## Test Timing

You are allowed two hours (120 minutes) to take the Praxis II® Elementary Education: Curriculum, Instruction, and Assessment test. There are 110 questions on the test, so you will have an average of about one minute to answer each question. The subject-specific sections within the test are not timed. That means you can spend more time on one section of the test than another.

## PACE YOURSELF

Remember: If you need to spend an extra 10 minutes on the math questions, for example, then you will simply need to spend 10 minutes less on one or more other sections.

You will not be allowed to leave the test center before the two hours are over. If you find that you have completed the test with time to spare, use the extra time to review your work. A valuable use of extra time is to recheck your calculations on the math problems. Above all else, make sure that you have answered every question. You may have decided to skip a hard problem and come back to it later. Make sure you don't leave any question blank, as there is no penalty for guessing.

## Test Scoring

Each multiple-choice question has equal worth. There may be a few questions that won't count toward your score, but you won't know which those will be. There is no guessing penalty, which means you will not lose points for getting a question wrong. That means you should still guess on a question, even if you are not sure what the correct answer is.

Even though there are 110 questions, your final score is not based on 110 points. ETS counts the number of questions you answered correctly and then translates that number into a scaled score from 100 to 200. The median score on the test is 164. According to ETS, the average student scores between 151 and 176.

If you take the computer version of the test, you will receive your score right away, immediately after you have completed the exam. Your official score will then be reported to you and the organizations you designate about two to three weeks after your test date.

If you take the paper version of the test, you will receive your score about a month after your test date. You can get your test score a few days earlier by using ETS's Scores by Phone service, but this convenience will cost you an additional $30.

## Registering for the Test

You can register for both the paper (0011) and computer (5011) versions of the Praxis II® Elementary Education: Curriculum, Instruction, and Assessment test online at www.ets.org/praxis/register. On the site, you can also check test dates and center locations most convenient to you. You can register for the computerized test electronically using a credit or debit card, and for the paper test by mailing in a hard copy form with a check or credit/debit card information.

## What to Bring to the Praxis®

You will need to bring identification and your admission ticket to your Praxis II® assessment. If you aren't taking the computerized test, be sure also to bring several sharpened #2 pencils with erasers. You will not be allowed to use a cell phone or other electronic device.

## Special Accommodations for the Praxis® Tests

ETS offers some accommodations for students with disabilities. For example, students may have extended time or additional rest breaks. Some students may take the Praxis II® test in a large print, Braille, or audio format.

You can view the testing arrangements and registration procedures at www.ets.org/praxis/prxdsabl .html. To find out if you are eligible for the special accommodations, you can contact ETS Disability Services directly:

Phone: Monday through Friday 8:30 A.M. to
5:00 P.M. Eastern Time
1-866-387-8602 (toll free) from the United States,
U.S. territories, and Canada
1-609-771-7780 (all other locations)
TTY: 1-609-771-7714
Fax: 1-609-771-7165
E-mail: stassd@ets.org
Mail: ETS Disability Services
P.O. Box 6054
Princeton, NJ 08541-6054

## How to Use This Book

Chapter 2 contains the LearningExpress Test Preparation System. Even if you feel confident about certain subject areas and don't feel that you need to read this entire book and take all the practice tests, make sure you read this chapter.

Chapter 3 contains the first full-length Praxis II® Elementary Education: Curriculum, Instruction, and Assessment diagnostic test. Set aside two hours to take this test when you are free from distractions. Turn off your phone, and take the test in one sitting. When you are finished, check your answers and read the explanations for the problems. You can use the results to determine in which areas you need to spend the most time reviewing content before you move on to the next practice test, and eventually the actual exam.

Chapters 4 and 5 contain two more full-length Praxis II® Elementary Education: Curriculum, Instruction, and Assessment practice tests with explanations. Just as you did with Practice Test 1, take these practice tests in a similar environment to the actual test. Time yourself so that you have exactly two hours to take the exam. Remove all distractions so you can focus on the test for two hours. When you've completed each practice test, review the answers and read the explanations. Then, return to your classroom or other study materials to review and master those specific subjects that are giving you the most trouble.

You're on the way to becoming a teacher—congratulations and good luck!

# THE LEARNING-EXPRESS TEST PREPARATION SYSTEM

## CHAPTER SUMMARY

The Praxis® series of tests can be challenging. A great deal of preparation is necessary for achieving top scores and advancing your career. The LearningExpress Test Preparation System, developed by leading experts exclusively for LearningExpress, offers strategies for developing the discipline and attitude required for success.

Fact: Taking the Praxis II® Elementary Education: Curriculum, Instruction, and Assessment test is not easy, and neither is getting ready for it. Your future career as a teacher depends on getting a passing score, but an assortment of pitfalls can keep you from doing your best. Here are some of the obstacles that can stand in the way of success:

- being unfamiliar with the exam format
- being paralyzed by test anxiety
- leaving your preparation to the last minute
- not preparing at all(!)
- not knowing vital test-taking skills: how to pace yourself through the exam, how to use the process of elimination, and when to guess
- not being in tip-top mental and physical shape
- messing up on test day by arriving late at the test site, having to work on an empty stomach, or feeling uncomfortable during the exam because the room is too hot or too cold

What's the common denominator in all these test-taking pitfalls? One thing: *control*. Who's in control, you or the exam?

Here's some good news: The LearningExpress Test Preparation System puts you in control. In nine easy-to-follow steps, you will learn everything you need to know to make sure that you are in charge of your preparation and your performance on the exam. Other test takers may let the tests get the better of them; other test takers may be unprepared or out of shape, but not you. You will have taken all the steps you need to take to get a high score on the Praxis II® Elementary Education: Curriculum, Instruction, and Assessment test.

Here's how the LearningExpress Test Preparation System works: Nine easy steps lead you through everything you need to know and do to get ready to master your exam. Each of the following steps includes both reading about the step and one or more activities. It's important that you do the activities along with the reading, or you won't be getting the full benefit of the system. Each step tells you approximately how much time that step will take you to complete.

| | |
|---|---|
| Step 1: Get Information | 50 minutes |
| Step 2: Conquer Test Anxiety | 20 minutes |
| Step 3: Make a Plan | 30 minutes |
| Step 4: Learn to Manage Your Time | 10 minutes |
| Step 5: Learn to Use the Process of Elimination | 20 minutes |
| Step 6: Know When to Guess | 20 minutes |
| Step 7: Reach Your Peak Performance Zone | 10 minutes |
| Step 8: Get Your Act Together | 10 minutes |
| Step 9: Do It! | 10 minutes |
| **Total** | **3 hours** |

We estimate that working through the entire system will take you approximately three hours, though it's perfectly okay if you work faster or slower.

If you take an afternoon or evening, you can work through the whole LearningExpress Test Preparation System in one sitting. Otherwise, you can break it up, and do just one or two steps a day for the next several days. It's up to you—remember, you are in control.

# Step 1: Get Information

**Time to complete: 50 minutes**
**Activity: Read Chapter 1, "About the Praxis II® Elementary Education: Curriculum, Instruction, and Assessment (0011/5011) Test."**

Knowledge is power. The first step in the LearningExpress Test Preparation System is finding out everything you can about the Praxis II® Elementary Education: Curriculum, Instruction, and Assessment test. Once you have your information, the next steps in the LearningExpress Test Preparation System will show you what to do about it.

## Part A: Straight Talk about the Praxis II® Elementary Education: Curriculum, Instruction, and Assessment Test

Why do you have to take a rigorous exam, anyway? It's simply an attempt to be sure you have the knowledge and skills necessary to be a teacher.

It's important for you to remember that your score on the Praxis® test does not determine how smart you are, or even whether you will make a good teacher. There are all kinds of things exams like these can't test, such as whether you have the drive, determination, and dedication to be a teacher. Those kinds of traits are hard to evaluate, while a test is easy to evaluate.

This is not to say that the exam is not important! The knowledge tested on the exam is knowledge you will need to do your job. And your ability to enter the profession you've trained for depends on passing.

And that's why you are here—using the LearningExpress Test Preparation System to achieve control over the exam.

## Part B: What's on the Test

If you haven't already done so, stop here and read Chapter 1, which gives you an overview of the exam. Then, go online and read the most up-to-date information about your exam directly from the test developers at www.ets.org/praxis.

# Step 2: Conquer Test Anxiety

**Time to complete: 20 minutes**
**Activity: Take the Test Anxiety Test.**

Having complete information about the exam is the first step in getting control over it. Next, you have to overcome one of the biggest obstacles to test success: test anxiety. Test anxiety not only impairs your performance on the exam, but also keeps you from preparing. In Step 2, you will learn stress management techniques that will help you succeed. Learn these strategies now, and practice them as you work through the practice tests so that they will be second nature to you by exam day.

## Combating Test Anxiety

The first thing you need to know is that a little test anxiety is a good thing. Everyone gets nervous before a big exam—and if that nervousness motivates you to prepare thoroughly, so much the better. It's said that Sir Laurence Olivier, one of the foremost British actors of the twentieth century, felt ill before every performance. His stage fright didn't impair his performance; in fact, it probably gave him a little extra edge—just the kind of edge you need to do well, whether on a stage or on an examination.

On page 12 is the Test Anxiety Test. Stop and answer the questions to find out whether your level of test anxiety is something you should worry about.

## Stress Management Before a Test

If you feel your level of anxiety getting the best of you in the weeks before a test, here is what you need to do to bring the level down again:

- **Get prepared.** There's nothing like knowing what to expect and being prepared for it to put you in control of test anxiety. That's why you are reading this book. Use it faithfully, and remind yourself that you are better prepared than most of the people taking the test.
- **Practice self-confidence.** A positive attitude is a great way to combat test anxiety. This is no time to be humble or shy. Stand in front of the mirror and say to your reflection, "I am prepared. I am full of self-confidence. I am going to ace this test. I know I can do it." Record it and play it back once a day. If you hear it often enough, you will believe it.
- **Fight negative messages.** Every time someone starts telling you how hard the exam is or how it's almost impossible to get a high score, tune the person out or ask him or her to not speak negatively around you. Don't listen to the negative messages. Turn on your recorder/player and listen to your self-confidence messages.
- **Visualize.** Imagine yourself reporting for duty on your first day as a teacher or in your teacher training program. Visualizing success can help make it happen—and it reminds you of why you are doing all this work preparing for the exam.
- **Exercise.** Physical activity helps calm your body down and focus your mind. Besides, being in good physical shape can actually help you do well on the exam. Go for a run, lift weights, go swimming—and do it regularly.

You need to worry about test anxiety only if it is extreme enough to impair your performance. The following questionnaire will provide a diagnosis of your level of test anxiety. In the blank before each statement, write the number that most accurately describes your experience.

0 = Never
1 = Once or twice
2 = Sometimes
3 = Often

\_\_\_ I have gotten so nervous before an exam that I simply put down the books and didn't study for it.

\_\_\_ I have experienced disabling physical symptoms such as vomiting and severe headaches because I was nervous about an exam.

\_\_\_ I have simply not shown up for an exam because I was afraid to take it.

\_\_\_ I have experienced dizziness and disorientation while taking an exam.

\_\_\_ I have had trouble filling in the little circles because my hands were shaking too hard.

\_\_\_ I have failed an exam because I was too nervous to complete it.

\_\_\_ **Total: Add up the numbers in the blanks.**

## *Your Test Stress Score*

Here are the steps you should take, depending on your score. If you scored:

- **Below 3**, your level of test anxiety is nothing to worry about; it's probably just enough to give you that little extra edge.

- **Between 3 and 6**, your test anxiety may be enough to impair your performance, and you should practice the stress management techniques in this section to try to bring your test anxiety down to manageable levels.

- **Above 6**, your level of test anxiety is a serious concern. In addition to practicing the stress management techniques listed in this section, you may want to seek additional, personal help. Call your local high school or community college and ask for the academic counselor. Tell the counselor that you have a level of test anxiety that sometimes keeps you from being able to take an exam. The counselor may be willing to help you or may suggest someone else you should talk to.

### Stress Management on Test Day

There are several ways you can bring down your level of anxiety on test day. They will work best if you practice them in the weeks before the test so that you know which ones work best for you.

- **Practice deep breathing.** Take a deep breath while you count to five. Hold it for a count of one, then let it out on a count of five. Repeat several times.
- **Move your body.** Try rolling your head in a circle. Rotate your shoulders. Shake your hands from the wrist. Many people find these movements very relaxing.
- **Visualize again.** Think of the place where you are most relaxed: lying on the beach in the sun, walking through the park, or wherever. Now close your eyes and imagine you are actually there. If you practice in advance, you will find that you need only a few seconds of this exercise to experience a significant increase in your sense of well-being.

When anxiety threatens to overwhelm you right there during the exam, there are still things you can do to manage your stress level:

- **Repeat your self-confidence messages.** You should have them memorized by now. Say them quietly to yourself, and believe them!
- **Visualize one more time.** This time, visualize yourself moving smoothly and quickly through the test, answering every question right and finishing just before time is up. Like most visualization techniques, this one works best if you have practiced it ahead of time.
- **Find an easy question.** Find an easy question, and answer it. Getting even one question finished gets you into the test-taking groove.
- **Take a mental break.** Everyone loses concentration once in a while during a long test. It's normal, so you shouldn't worry about it. Instead, accept what has happened. Say to yourself, "Hey, I lost it there for a minute. My brain is taking a break." Put down your pencil, close your eyes, and do some deep breathing for a few seconds. Then you are ready to go back to work.

Try these techniques ahead of time, and see whether they work for you!

## Step 3: Make a Plan

**Time to complete: 30 minutes**
**Activity: Construct a study plan.**

Maybe the most important thing you can do to get control of yourself and your exam is to make a study plan. Too many people fail to prepare simply because they fail to plan. Spending hours on the day before the exam poring over sample test questions not only raises your level of test anxiety, but also is simply no substitute for careful preparation and practice over time.

Don't fall into the cram trap. Take control of your preparation time by mapping out a study schedule. On the following pages are two sample schedules, based on the amount of time you have before you take the Praxis II® Elementary Education: Curriculum, Instruction, and Assessment test. If you are the kind of person who needs deadlines and assignments to motivate you for a project, here they are. If you are the kind of person who doesn't like to follow other people's plans, you can use the suggested schedules here to construct your own.

Even more important than making a plan is making a commitment. You have to set aside some time every day for study and practice. Try for at least 20 minutes a day. Twenty minutes daily will do you much more good than two hours on Saturday.

Don't put off your study until the day before the exam. Start now. A few minutes a day, with half an hour or more on weekends, can make a big difference in your score.

## Schedule A: The 30-Day Plan

If you have at least a month before you take the Praxis II® Elementary Education: Curriculum, Instruction, and Assessment test, you have plenty of time to prepare—as long as you don't waste it! If you have less than a month, turn to Schedule B.

| TIME | PREPARATION |
|---|---|
| Days 1–4 | Skim over any other study materials you may have. Make a note of areas you expect to be emphasized on the exam and areas you don't feel confident in. On Day 4, concentrate on those areas. |
| Day 5 | Take the first practice test in Chapter 3. Score the test, and identify two areas that you will concentrate on before you take the second practice exam. |
| Days 6–10 | Study one of the areas you identified as a weak point. Review your classroom or other study materials in detail to improve your score on the next practice test. |
| Days 11–14 | Study another area you identified as a weak point. Review your classroom or other study materials in detail to improve your score on the next practice test. |
| Day 15 | Take the second practice exam in Chapter 4. |
| Day 16 | Score the practice exam. Identify one area to concentrate on before you take the next practice exam. |
| Days 17–21 | Study the one area you identified for review. Again, review your classroom or other study materials in detail. |
| Day 22 | Take the third practice exam in Chapter 5. |
| Day 23 | Score the test. Note how much you have improved! |
| Days 24–28 | Study any remaining topics you still need to review. |
| Day 29 | Take an overview of all your study materials, consolidating your strengths and improving on any weaknesses. |
| Day before the exam | Relax. Do something unrelated to the exam, and go to bed at a reasonable hour. |

## *Schedule B: The Ten-Day Plan*

If you have two weeks or less before you take the test, use this ten-day schedule to help you make the most of your time.

| TIME | PREPARATION |
| --- | --- |
| Day 1 | Take the first practice test in Chapter 3, and score it, and note which topics you need to review most. |
| Day 2 | Study one of the areas you identified as a weak point. Review your classroom or other study materials in detail to improve your score on the next practice test. |
| Day 3 | Study another area you identified as a weak point. Review your classroom or other study materials in detail to improve your score on the next practice test. |
| Day 4 | Take the second practice exam in Chapter 4 and score it. |
| Day 5 | If your score on the second practice exam doesn't show improvement on the two areas you studied, review them. If you did improve in those areas, choose a new weak area to study today. |
| Days 6–7 | Continue to review your classroom or other study materials to improve some skills and reinforce others. |
| Day 8 | Take the third practice exam in Chapter 5 and score it. |
| Day 9 | Choose your weakest area from the third practice exam to review. |
| Day 10 | Use your last study day to brush up on any areas that are still giving you trouble. |
| Day before the exam | Relax. Do something unrelated to the exam, and go to bed at a reasonable hour. |

## Step 4: Learn to Manage Your Time

**Time to complete: 10 minutes to read, many hours of practice!**

**Activity: Practice these strategies as you take the sample tests in this book.**

Steps 4, 5, and 6 of the LearningExpress Test Preparation System put you in charge of your exam by showing you test-taking strategies that work. Practice these strategies as you take the sample tests, and then you will be ready to use them on test day.

First, take control of your time on the exam. It's a terrible feeling to know there are only five minutes left when you are only three-quarters of the way through a test. Here are some tips to keep that from happening to you:

- **Follow directions.** You should take your time making your way through the computer tutorial before the exam. Read the directions carefully and ask questions before the exam begins if there's anything you don't understand.
- **Pace yourself.** If there is a timer on the screen as you take the exam, keep an eye on it. This will help you pace yourself. For example, when one-quarter of the time has elapsed, you should be a quarter of the way through the test, and so on. If you are falling behind, pick up the pace a bit.
- **Keep moving.** Don't waste time on one question. If you don't know the answer, skip the question and move on. You can always go back to it later.
- **Don't rush.** Although you should keep moving, rushing won't help. Try to keep calm and work methodically and quickly.

## Step 5: Learn to Use the Process of Elimination

**Time to complete: 20 minutes**

**Activity: Complete the Using the Process of Elimination worksheet**

After time management, your next most important tool for taking control of your exam is using the process of elimination wisely. It's standard test-taking wisdom that you should always read all the answer choices before choosing your answer. This helps you find the right answer by eliminating wrong answer choices. And, sure enough, that standard wisdom applies to your exam, too.

You should always use the process of elimination on tough questions, even if the right answer jumps out at you. Sometimes the answer that jumps out isn't right after all. You should always proceed through the answer choices in order. You can start with answer choice **a**, and eliminate any choices that are clearly incorrect.

Even when you think you are absolutely clueless about a question, you can often use the process of elimination to get rid of one answer choice. If so, you are better prepared to make an educated guess, as you will see in Step 6. More often, the process of elimination allows you to get down to only two possibly right answers. Then you are in a strong position to guess. And sometimes, even though you don't know the right answer, you find it simply by getting rid of the wrong ones.

Try using your powers of elimination on the questions in the worksheet on Using the Process of Elimination. The questions aren't about teaching; they're just designed to show you how the process of elimination works. The answer explanations for this worksheet show one possible way that you might use the process to arrive at the right answer.

The process of elimination is your tool for the next step, which is knowing when to guess.

# USING THE PROCESS OF ELIMINATION

Use the process of elimination to answer the following questions.

1. Ilsa is as old as Meghan will be in five years. The difference between Ed's age and Meghan's age is twice the difference between Ilsa's age and Meghan's age. Ed is 29. How old is Ilsa?
   a. 4
   b. 10
   c. 19
   d. 24

2. "All drivers of commercial vehicles must carry a valid commercial driver's license whenever operating a commercial vehicle."

   According to this sentence, which of the following people need NOT carry a commercial driver's license?
   a. a truck driver idling his engine while waiting to be directed to a loading dock
   b. a bus operator backing her bus out of the way of another bus in the bus lot
   c. a taxi driver driving his personal car to the grocery store
   d. a limousine driver taking the limousine to her home after dropping off her last passenger of the evening

3. Smoking tobacco has been linked to
   a. increased risk of stroke and heart attack.
   b. all forms of respiratory disease.
   c. increasing mortality rates over the past 10 years.
   d. juvenile delinquency.

4. Which of the following words is spelled correctly?
   a. incorrigible
   b. outragous
   c. domestickated
   d. understandible

## Answers

Here are the answers, as well as some suggestions as to how you might use the process of elimination to find them.

1. d. You should eliminate choice a right off the bat. Ilsa can't be four years old if Meghan is going to be Ilsa's age in five years. The best way to eliminate other answer choices is to try plugging them in to the information given in the problem. For instance, for choice b, if Ilsa is 10, then Meghan must be 5. The difference between their ages is five years. The difference between Ed's age, 29, and Meghan's age, 5, is 24. Is 24 two times 5? No. Then choice b is wrong. You could eliminate choice c in the same way and be left with choice d.

2. c. Note the word *not* in the question, and go through the answers one by one. Is the truck driver in choice a "operating a commercial vehicle"? Yes, idling counts as "operating," so he needs to have a commercial driver's license. Likewise, the bus operator in choice b is operating a commercial vehicle; the question doesn't say the operator has to be on the street. The limo driver in choice d is operating a commercial vehicle, even though it doesn't have a passenger in it. However, the driver in choice c is *not* operating a commercial vehicle, but his own private car.

**3. a.** You could eliminate choice **b** simply because of the presence of the word *all*. Such absolutes hardly ever appear in correct answer choices. Choice **c** looks attractive until you think a little about what you know—aren't fewer people smoking these days, rather than more? So how could smoking be responsible for increasing mortality rates? (If you didn't know that *mortality rate* means the rate at which people die, you might keep this choice as a possibility, but you would still be able to eliminate two answers and have only two to choose from.) And choice **d** is plain silly, so you could eliminate that one, too. You are left with the correct choice, **a.**

**4. a.** How you use the process of elimination here depends on which words you recognize as being spelled incorrectly. If you knew that the correct spellings are *outrageous*, *domesticated*, and *understandable*, then you would be home free. You probably know that at least one of those words was spelled wrong in the question.

# YOUR GUESSING ABILITY

The following are ten really hard questions. You are not supposed to know the answers. Rather, this is an assessment of your ability to guess when you don't have a clue. Read each question carefully, as if you were expected to answer it. If you have any knowledge of the subject, use that knowledge to help you eliminate wrong answer choices.

| | | | | | | | | | | | | | |
|---|---|---|---|---|---|---|---|---|---|---|---|---|---|
| **1.** | ⓐ | ⓑ | ⓒ | ⓓ | **5.** | ⓐ | ⓑ | ⓒ | ⓓ | **9.** | ⓐ | ⓑ | ⓒ ⓓ |
| **2.** | ⓐ | ⓑ | ⓒ | ⓓ | **6.** | ⓐ | ⓑ | ⓒ | ⓓ | **10.** | ⓐ | ⓑ | ⓒ ⓓ |
| **3.** | ⓐ | ⓑ | ⓒ | ⓓ | **7.** | ⓐ | ⓑ | ⓒ | ⓓ | | | | |
| **4.** | ⓐ | ⓑ | ⓒ | ⓓ | **8.** | ⓐ | ⓑ | ⓒ | ⓓ | | | | |

**1.** September 7 is Independence Day in
  **a.** India.
  **b.** Costa Rica.
  **c.** Brazil.
  **d.** Australia.

**2.** Which of the following is the formula for determining the momentum of an object?
  **a.** $p = MV$
  **b.** $F = ma$
  **c.** $P = IV$
  **d.** $E = mc^2$

**3.** Because of the expansion of the universe, the stars and other celestial bodies are all moving away from each other. This phenomenon is known as
  **a.** Newton's first law.
  **b.** the big bang.
  **c.** gravitational collapse.
  **d.** Hubble flow.

**4.** American author Gertrude Stein was born in
  **a.** 1713.
  **b.** 1830.
  **c.** 1874.
  **d.** 1901.

**5.** Which of the following is NOT one of the Five Classics attributed to Confucius?
  **a.** *I Ching*
  **b.** *Book of Holiness*
  **c.** *Spring and Autumn Annals*
  **d.** *Book of History*

**6.** The religious and philosophical doctrine that holds that the universe is constantly in a struggle between good and evil is known as
  **a.** Pelagianism.
  **b.** Manichaeanism.
  **c.** neo-Hegelianism.
  **d.** Epicureanism.

7. The third chief justice of the U.S. Supreme Court was
   a. John Blair.
   b. William Cushing.
   c. James Wilson.
   d. John Jay.

8. Which of the following is the poisonous portion of a daffodil?
   a. the bulb
   b. the leaves
   c. the stem
   d. the flowers

9. The winner of the Masters golf tournament in 1953 was
   a. Sam Snead.
   b. Cary Middlecoff.
   c. Arnold Palmer.
   d. Ben Hogan.

10. The state with the highest per capita personal income in 1980 was
    a. Alaska.
    b. Connecticut.
    c. New York.
    d. Texas.

## Answers

Check your answers against the following correct answers.

1. c
2. a
3. d
4. c
5. b
6. b
7. b
8. a
9. d
10. a

## How Did You Do?

You may have simply gotten lucky and actually known the answer to one or two questions. In addition, your guessing was probably more successful if you were able to use the process of elimination on any of the questions. Maybe you didn't know who the third Chief Justice was (question 7), but you knew that John Jay was the first. In that case, you would have eliminated choice **d** and, therefore, improved your odds of guessing right from one in four to one in three.

According to probability, you should get 2.5 answers correct, so getting either two or three right would be average. If you got four or more right, you may be a really terrific guesser. If you got one or none right, you may need to work on your guessing skills.

Keep in mind, though, that this is only a small sample. You should continue to keep track of your guessing ability as you work through the sample questions in this book. Circle the numbers of questions you guess on as you make your guess; or, if you don't have time while you take the practice tests, go back afterward and try to remember which questions you guessed at. Remember, on a test with four answer choices, your chance of guessing correctly is one in four. So keep a separate guessing score for each exam. How many questions did you guess on? How many did you get right? If the number you got right is at least one-fourth of the number of questions you guessed on, you are at least an average guesser—maybe better—and you should always go ahead and guess on the real exam. If the number you got right is significantly lower than one-fourth of the number you guessed on, you would be safe in guessing anyway, but maybe you would feel more comfortable if you guessed only selectively, when you can eliminate a wrong answer or at least have a good feeling about one of the answer choices.

Remember, even if you are a play-it-safe person with lousy intuition, you are still safe guessing every time.

## Step 6: Know When to Guess

**Time to complete: 20 minutes**
**Activity: Complete the worksheet on Your**
**Guessing Ability.**

Armed with the process of elimination, you are ready to take control of one of the big questions in test taking: Should I guess? The answer is: *Yes.* Some exams have what's called a "guessing penalty," in which a fraction of your wrong answers is subtracted from your right answers—but the Praxis® series of tests does *not* work like that. The number of questions you answer correctly yields your raw score. So you have nothing to lose and everything to gain by guessing.

## Step 7: Reach Your Peak Performance Zone

**Time to complete: 10 minutes to read; weeks to**
**complete!**
**Activity: Complete the Physical Preparation**
**Checklist.**

To get ready for a challenge like a big exam, you have to take control of your physical, as well as your mental, state. Exercise, proper diet, and rest will ensure that your body works with, rather than against, your mind on test day, as well as during your preparation.

### Exercise

If you don't already have a regular exercise program going, the time during which you are preparing for an exam is actually an excellent time to start one. And if you are already keeping fit—or trying to get that way—don't let the pressure of preparing for an exam fool you into quitting now. Exercise helps reduce stress by pumping wonderful good-feeling hormones called *endorphins* into your system. It also increases the oxygen supply throughout your body, including

your brain, so you will be at peak performance on test day.

A half hour of vigorous activity—enough to raise a sweat—every day should be your aim. If you are really pressed for time, every other day is okay. Choose an activity you like and get out there and do it. Jogging with a friend always makes the time go faster, or take a radio or music player.

But don't overdo it. You don't want to exhaust yourself. Moderation is the key.

### Diet

First of all, cut out the junk food. Go easy on caffeine and nicotine, and eliminate alcohol and any other drugs from your system at least two weeks before the exam. Promise yourself a treat the night after the exam, if need be.

What your body needs for peak performance is simply a balanced diet. Eat plenty of fruits and vegetables, along with protein and carbohydrates. Foods that are high in lecithin (an amino acid), such as fish and beans, are especially good brain foods.

The night before the exam, you might carbo-load the way athletes do before a contest. Eat a big plate of spaghetti, rice and beans, or whatever your favorite carbohydrate is.

### Rest

You probably know how much sleep you need every night to be at your best, even if you don't always get it. Make sure you do get that much sleep, though, for at least a week before the exam. Moderation is important here, too. Extra sleep will just make you groggy.

If you are not a morning person and your exam will be given in the morning, you should reset your internal clock so that your body doesn't think you are taking an exam at 3 A.M. You have to start this process well before the exam. The way it works is to get up half an hour earlier each morning, and then go to bed half an hour earlier that night. Don't try it the other way around; you will just toss and turn if you go to bed early without having gotten up early. The next morning, get up another half an hour earlier, and so on. How long you will have to do this depends on how late you are used to getting up. Use the Physical Preparation Checklist on the next page to make sure you are in tip-top form.

## Step 8: Get Your Act Together

**Time to complete: 10 minutes to read; time to complete will vary**
**Activity: Complete the Final Preparations worksheet.**

You are in control of your mind and body, which means you are in charge of test anxiety, your preparation, and your test-taking strategies. Now it's time to take charge of external factors, like the testing site and the materials you need to take to the exam.

### Find Out Where the Exam Is, and Make a Trial Run

Do you know how to get to the testing site? Do you know how long it will take to get there? If not, make a trial run, preferably on the same day of the week at the same time of day as when you will be taking your test. Note on the Final Preparations worksheet on the next page the amount of time it will take you to get to the exam site. Plan on arriving 30 to 45 minutes early so you can get the lay of the land, use the bathroom, and calm down. Then figure out how early you will have to get up that morning, and make sure you get up that early every day for a week before the exam.

### Gather Your Materials

The night before the exam, lay out the clothes you will wear and the materials you have to bring with you to the exam. Plan on dressing in layers; you won't have any control over the temperature of the examination room. Have a sweater or jacket that you can take off if it's warm. Use the checklist on the Final Preparations worksheet to help you pull together what you will need.

### Don't Skip Breakfast

Even if you don't usually eat breakfast, do so on exam morning. A cup of coffee doesn't count. Don't eat doughnuts or other sweet foods, either. A sugar high will leave you with a sugar low in the middle of the exam. A mix of protein and carbohydrates is best: Cereal with milk and just a little sugar, or eggs with toast, will do your body a world of good.

## Step 9: Do It!

**Time to complete: 10 minutes, plus test-taking time**
**Activity: Ace the exam!**

Fast-forward to exam day. You are ready. You made a study plan and followed through. You practiced your test-taking strategies. You are in control of your physical, mental, and emotional state. You know when and where to show up and what to bring with you. In other words, you are better prepared than most of the other people taking the exam. You are psyched.

Just one more thing: When you are finished with the exam, you will have earned a reward. Plan a celebration. Call up your friends and plan a party, or have a nice dinner for two—whatever your heart desires. Give yourself something to look forward to.

And then do it. Go into the exam full of confidence and armed with test-taking strategies you have practiced until they're second nature. You are in control of yourself, your environment, and your performance on the exam. You are ready to succeed. So do it. Go in there and ace the exam. And look forward to your future career as a teacher!

# PHYSICAL PREPARATION CHECKLIST

For the week before the exam, write down what physical exercise you engaged in and for how long and what you ate for each meal. Remember, you are trying for at least half an hour of exercise every other day (preferably every day) and a balanced diet that is light on junk food.

## Exam minus 7 days

Exercise: _____ for _____ minutes

Breakfast: _____

Lunch: _____

Dinner: _____

Snacks: _____

## Exam minus 6 days

Exercise: _____ for _____ minutes

Breakfast: _____

Lunch: _____

Dinner: _____

Snacks: _____

## Exam minus 5 days

Exercise: _____ for _____ minutes

Breakfast: _____

Lunch: _____

Dinner: _____

Snacks: _____

## Exam minus 4 days

Exercise: _____ for _____ minutes

Breakfast: _____

Lunch: _____

Dinner: _____

Snacks: _____

## Exam minus 3 days

Exercise: _____ for _____ minutes

Breakfast: _____

Lunch: _____

Dinner: _____

Snacks: _____

## Exam minus 2 days

Exercise: _____ for _____ minutes

Breakfast: _____

Lunch: _____

Dinner: _____

Snacks: _____

## Exam minus 1 day

Exercise: _____ for _____ minutes

Breakfast: _____

Lunch: _____

Dinner: _____

Snacks: _____

## Getting to the Exam Site

Location of exam site: _____

Date: _____

Departure time: _____

Do I know how to get to the exam site?   Yes ___   No ___   (If no, make a trial run.)

Time it will take to get to the exam site: _____

## Things to Lay Out the Night Before

Clothes I will wear          _____

Sweater/jacket              _____

Watch                      _____

Photo ID                   _____

Admission ticket           _____

Four #2 pencils and
blue or black ink pens
(if taking the paper-
based test)                _____

## Other Things to Bring/Remember

*(Do not bring electronic devices into the testing site.)*

_____

_____

_____

_____

_____

_____

_____

_____

# 3 ▶ ELEMENTARY EDUCATION: CURRICULUM, INSTRUCTION, AND ASSESSMENT PRACTICE TEST 1

### CHAPTER SUMMARY

This is the first of the three full-length exams based on the structure and difficulty level of the Praxis II® Elementary Education: Curriculum, Instruction, and Assessment test. Use this test to see how you would do if you were to take the exam today.

T his chapter contains a practice test that mirrors the Praxis II® Elementary Education: Curriculum, Instruction, and Assessment test. Though the actual exam you will take might be computer-based, the question types for each exam are replicated here for you in the book.

As you take this first test, do not worry too much about timing. The actual time you will be allotted for each exam is at the beginning of each test, but you should take Practice Test 1 in as relaxed a manner as you can to find out in which areas you are skilled and in which ones you will need extra work.

After you finish taking your test, you should review the answer explanations. (Each individual test is followed by its own answer explanations.) See the Note on Scoring after the final answer explanation to find information on how to score your exam.

Good luck!

| | | | | | | | | | | | | | | |
|---|---|---|---|---|---|---|---|---|---|---|---|---|---|---|
| 1. | ⓐ | ⓑ | ⓒ | ⓓ | 38. | ⓐ | ⓑ | ⓒ | ⓓ | 75. | ⓐ | ⓑ | ⓒ | ⓓ |
| 2. | ⓐ | ⓑ | ⓒ | ⓓ | 39. | ⓐ | ⓑ | ⓒ | ⓓ | 76. | ⓐ | ⓑ | ⓒ | ⓓ |
| 3. | ⓐ | ⓑ | ⓒ | ⓓ | 40. | ⓐ | ⓑ | ⓒ | ⓓ | 77. | ⓐ | ⓑ | ⓒ | ⓓ |
| 4. | ⓐ | ⓑ | ⓒ | ⓓ | 41. | ⓐ | ⓑ | ⓒ | ⓓ | 78. | ⓐ | ⓑ | ⓒ | ⓓ |
| 5. | ⓐ | ⓑ | ⓒ | ⓓ | 42. | ⓐ | ⓑ | ⓒ | ⓓ | 79. | ⓐ | ⓑ | ⓒ | ⓓ |
| 6. | ⓐ | ⓑ | ⓒ | ⓓ | 43. | ⓐ | ⓑ | ⓒ | ⓓ | 80. | ⓐ | ⓑ | ⓒ | ⓓ |
| 7. | ⓐ | ⓑ | ⓒ | ⓓ | 44. | ⓐ | ⓑ | ⓒ | ⓓ | 81. | ⓐ | ⓑ | ⓒ | ⓓ |
| 8. | ⓐ | ⓑ | ⓒ | ⓓ | 45. | ⓐ | ⓑ | ⓒ | ⓓ | 82. | ⓐ | ⓑ | ⓒ | ⓓ |
| 9. | ⓐ | ⓑ | ⓒ | ⓓ | 46. | ⓐ | ⓑ | ⓒ | ⓓ | 83. | ⓐ | ⓑ | ⓒ | ⓓ |
| 10. | ⓐ | ⓑ | ⓒ | ⓓ | 47. | ⓐ | ⓑ | ⓒ | ⓓ | 84. | ⓐ | ⓑ | ⓒ | ⓓ |
| 11. | ⓐ | ⓑ | ⓒ | ⓓ | 48. | ⓐ | ⓑ | ⓒ | ⓓ | 85. | ⓐ | ⓑ | ⓒ | ⓓ |
| 12. | ⓐ | ⓑ | ⓒ | ⓓ | 49. | ⓐ | ⓑ | ⓒ | ⓓ | 86. | ⓐ | ⓑ | ⓒ | ⓓ |
| 13. | ⓐ | ⓑ | ⓒ | ⓓ | 50. | ⓐ | ⓑ | ⓒ | ⓓ | 87. | ⓐ | ⓑ | ⓒ | ⓓ |
| 14. | ⓐ | ⓑ | ⓒ | ⓓ | 51. | ⓐ | ⓑ | ⓒ | ⓓ | 88. | ⓐ | ⓑ | ⓒ | ⓓ |
| 15. | ⓐ | ⓑ | ⓒ | ⓓ | 52. | ⓐ | ⓑ | ⓒ | ⓓ | 89. | ⓐ | ⓑ | ⓒ | ⓓ |
| 16. | ⓐ | ⓑ | ⓒ | ⓓ | 53. | ⓐ | ⓑ | ⓒ | ⓓ | 90. | ⓐ | ⓑ | ⓒ | ⓓ |
| 17. | ⓐ | ⓑ | ⓒ | ⓓ | 54. | ⓐ | ⓑ | ⓒ | ⓓ | 91. | ⓐ | ⓑ | ⓒ | ⓓ |
| 18. | ⓐ | ⓑ | ⓒ | ⓓ | 55. | ⓐ | ⓑ | ⓒ | ⓓ | 92. | ⓐ | ⓑ | ⓒ | ⓓ |
| 19. | ⓐ | ⓑ | ⓒ | ⓓ | 56. | ⓐ | ⓑ | ⓒ | ⓓ | 93. | ⓐ | ⓑ | ⓒ | ⓓ |
| 20. | ⓐ | ⓑ | ⓒ | ⓓ | 57. | ⓐ | ⓑ | ⓒ | ⓓ | 94. | ⓐ | ⓑ | ⓒ | ⓓ |
| 21. | ⓐ | ⓑ | ⓒ | ⓓ | 58. | ⓐ | ⓑ | ⓒ | ⓓ | 95. | ⓐ | ⓑ | ⓒ | ⓓ |
| 22. | ⓐ | ⓑ | ⓒ | ⓓ | 59. | ⓐ | ⓑ | ⓒ | ⓓ | 96. | ⓐ | ⓑ | ⓒ | ⓓ |
| 23. | ⓐ | ⓑ | ⓒ | ⓓ | 60. | ⓐ | ⓑ | ⓒ | ⓓ | 97. | ⓐ | ⓑ | ⓒ | ⓓ |
| 24. | ⓐ | ⓑ | ⓒ | ⓓ | 61. | ⓐ | ⓑ | ⓒ | ⓓ | 98. | ⓐ | ⓑ | ⓒ | ⓓ |
| 25. | ⓐ | ⓑ | ⓒ | ⓓ | 62. | ⓐ | ⓑ | ⓒ | ⓓ | 99. | ⓐ | ⓑ | ⓒ | ⓓ |
| 26. | ⓐ | ⓑ | ⓒ | ⓓ | 63. | ⓐ | ⓑ | ⓒ | ⓓ | 100. | ⓐ | ⓑ | ⓒ | ⓓ |
| 27. | ⓐ | ⓑ | ⓒ | ⓓ | 64. | ⓐ | ⓑ | ⓒ | ⓓ | 101. | ⓐ | ⓑ | ⓒ | ⓓ |
| 28. | ⓐ | ⓑ | ⓒ | ⓓ | 65. | ⓐ | ⓑ | ⓒ | ⓓ | 102. | ⓐ | ⓑ | ⓒ | ⓓ |
| 29. | ⓐ | ⓑ | ⓒ | ⓓ | 66. | ⓐ | ⓑ | ⓒ | ⓓ | 103. | ⓐ | ⓑ | ⓒ | ⓓ |
| 30. | ⓐ | ⓑ | ⓒ | ⓓ | 67. | ⓐ | ⓑ | ⓒ | ⓓ | 104. | ⓐ | ⓑ | ⓒ | ⓓ |
| 31. | ⓐ | ⓑ | ⓒ | ⓓ | 68. | ⓐ | ⓑ | ⓒ | ⓓ | 105. | ⓐ | ⓑ | ⓒ | ⓓ |
| 32. | ⓐ | ⓑ | ⓒ | ⓓ | 69. | ⓐ | ⓑ | ⓒ | ⓓ | 106. | ⓐ | ⓑ | ⓒ | ⓓ |
| 33. | ⓐ | ⓑ | ⓒ | ⓓ | 70. | ⓐ | ⓑ | ⓒ | ⓓ | 107. | ⓐ | ⓑ | ⓒ | ⓓ |
| 34. | ⓐ | ⓑ | ⓒ | ⓓ | 71. | ⓐ | ⓑ | ⓒ | ⓓ | 108. | ⓐ | ⓑ | ⓒ | ⓓ |
| 35. | ⓐ | ⓑ | ⓒ | ⓓ | 72. | ⓐ | ⓑ | ⓒ | ⓓ | 109. | ⓐ | ⓑ | ⓒ | ⓓ |
| 36. | ⓐ | ⓑ | ⓒ | ⓓ | 73. | ⓐ | ⓑ | ⓒ | ⓓ | 110. | ⓐ | ⓑ | ⓒ | ⓓ |
| 37. | ⓐ | ⓑ | ⓒ | ⓓ | 74. | ⓐ | ⓑ | ⓒ | ⓓ | | | | | |

**Time—120 minutes**
**110 Questions**

**Directions:** Each of the questions or incomplete statements that follow is followed by four suggested answers or completions. Select the one that is best in each case and fill in the corresponding lettered space on the answer sheet with a heavy, dark mark so that you cannot see the letter.

# Reading and Language Arts

**1.** A teacher writes out the following sentences:

*What type of figurative language is shown in the following sentence?*

*Miserly Matt must make more money.*

What type of figurative language is the teacher teaching?
**a.** alliteration
**b.** onomatopoeia
**c.** simile
**d.** metaphor

**2.** A teacher gives the student a reading passage like the following:

*Last weekend Elianna was so excited about playing on the beach. She played in the water, built sandcastles, and picked up seashells. Because she forgot to put on sunscreen, at the end of the day she felt very hot, and her skin was as red as fire; she couldn't stand to touch it. She was sunburned!*

*What caused Elianna to get sunburned?*

What text structure is the teacher teaching?
**a.** cause and effect
**b.** sequencing
**c.** compare and contrast
**d.** main idea and details

**3.** Which Common Core standard applies to answering this question?

*"Here's the key," she would say, **retrieving** a small brass key from her pocket.*

*What is a synonym for the word* retrieving?
**a.** Use context as a clue to the meaning of a word or phrase.
**b.** Interpret figures of speech.
**c.** Use knowledge of language and its conventions when writing, speaking, reading, or listening.
**d.** Distinguish among the connotations (associations) of words with similar denotations (definitions).

**4.** What can a teacher do to see if the students in the class have the ability to detect rhyming words?
**a.** Have the students manipulate the parts of words (for example, change the /th/ of *thing* to /s/, /cl/, and /w/ to form *sing, cling,* and *wing*).
**b.** Have the students tap out and count various words.
**c.** Have students complete a word when only part is given (for example, say *table* when the first part only is said, e.g., "ta—").
**d.** Have students segment phonemes.

**5.** To raise a learner's awareness of letter recognition, a teacher could use all of the following strategies EXCEPT
**a.** games and activities where learners circle the target letters.
**b.** letter bingo using uppercase and lowercase letters.
**c.** introducing initial and final blends of words.
**d.** identifying individual letters or words.

**6.** In a lesson a teacher had the students read a text, and one of the sentences was "*One becquerel is defined as one transformation (or decay) per second.*" The students did not understand the vocabulary word *transformation*. What strategy could the teacher use to help the students understand the unknown word?
**a.** predicting
**b.** visualizing
**c.** questioning
**d.** building background knowledge

**7.** A teacher gives the students in the class the following question:

*Choose an animal or object you might find in the zoo and find information about the animal or object and write a report about it.*

What type of writing is the teacher asking the students to compose?
**a.** personal narrative
**b.** persuasive
**c.** informational
**d.** journaling

**8.** Which of the following is NOT an appropriate tool for formative assessment?
**a.** assignment
**b.** oral questions
**c.** midterm test
**d.** quizzes and games

**9.** Which of the following cannot be tested using a summative assessment?
**a.** reading for information
**b.** meaning of words and phrases
**c.** reading for pleasure
**d.** analyzing texts

**10.** When scaffolding for struggling readers, a teacher recognizes that giving a word bank and brainstorming helps students to build
**a.** vocabulary.
**b.** ideas.
**c.** writing skills.
**d.** reading comprehension.

**11.** Grammar should be taught by
**a.** asking students to learn the rules.
**b.** making learners do written assignments.
**c.** giving clear explanations and examples.
**d.** enabling practice in context.

**12.** A teacher uses "big books" in the classroom during reading. What is the purpose of using these "big books"?
**a.** to allow students to read at home
**b.** to ensure books have a lot of information
**c.** to use the books to perform shared reading
**d.** to use the books to perform shared writing

**13.** Students who are asked to prewrite, draft, edit, and revise work show a process that reflects
**a.** reading skills.
**b.** writing skills.
**c.** listening skills.
**d.** speaking skills.

**14.** Cooperative work allows students to develop
**a.** healthy competition among the students.
**b.** good memories.
**c.** a high level of ambition to achieve.
**d.** collaboration, critical thinking, and problem solving.

**15.** A teacher gives the students a book to read where the stories are grounded in history and the setting is an authentic part of the story. The characters' actions, dialogue, and beliefs are based on a work of fiction, although they are true to the historical period. What type of text are the students reading?
**a.** realistic fiction
**b.** historical fiction
**c.** science fiction
**d.** informational

**16.** When designing a lesson for instructional modifications for the students in the classroom, a teacher should ask himself or herself all of the following EXCEPT which question?
**a.** Does the modification provide for student participation?
**b.** Does the modification build on learner abilities and interests?
**c.** Does the modification allow the student to find where his or her weaknesses lie?
**d.** Does the modification allow for greater student success?

**17.** A school is investigating how the results of state and local assessments can be used to strengthen curriculum and instruction. What type of assessments is the school looking at to help its students?
**a.** summative assessments
**b.** formative assessments
**c.** alternative assessments
**d.** interim assessments

**18.** The following graphic organizer is an example of a

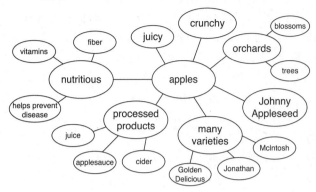

**a.** story map.
**b.** semantic map.
**c.** K-W-L chart.
**d.** T-chart.

**19.** A teacher's lesson plans state that the instructional outcome is to have students use academic language in the class during the lesson. Which Common Core state standard is the teacher addressing?
**a.** Prepare for and participate effectively in a range of conversations and collaborations with diverse partners, building on others' ideas and expressing students' own ideas clearly and persuasively.
**b.** Integrate and evaluate information presented in diverse media and formats, including visually, quantitatively, and orally.
**c.** Evaluate a speaker's point of view, reasoning, and use of evidence and rhetoric.
**d.** Make strategic use of digital media and visual displays of data to express information and enhance understanding of presentations.

**20.** A teacher has several English language learners (ELLs) in the classroom. The teacher wants to allow the students to complete a close reading of a complex text. The teacher can do all of the following to modify the same lesson for the ELLs EXCEPT
   **a.** engage in multiple readings of the text.
   **b.** shorten and take out difficult vocabulary from the text.
   **c.** give supplementary questions to help students comprehend.
   **d.** give sentence starters and word banks to help answer the questions.

**21.** To provide student-directed learning for vocabulary instruction, a teacher could
   **a.** supply glossaries.
   **b.** provide definitions in context.
   **c.** use gestures to demonstrate a word.
   **d.** illustrate the word.

**22.** What does it mean when a student has phonemic awareness?
   **a.** phonological awareness where words can be divided into syllables
   **b.** phonological awareness where a student can hear phonemes in words
   **c.** phonological awareness where a student understands that words share a rime unit
   **d.** the ability to hear and work with sounds in words

**23.** A teacher uses Elkonin boxes with the kindergarten students in the class. The purposes of using them are all of the following EXCEPT which one?
   **a.** They help students build phonological awareness by segmenting words into sounds or syllables.
   **b.** They teach students how to count the number of phonemes in the word (not always the number of letters).
   **c.** They help students better understand the alphabetic principle in decoding and spelling.
   **d.** They help students build a well-developed listening vocabulary.

**24.** A student comes from Africa, where she had never attended school. The student is having difficulty holding a pencil and knowing where to place her pencil on the paper. To help the student with letter formation, the teacher can
   **a.** provide the student with different media for making letters (e.g., large pencil, whiteboard, computer, or paints).
   **b.** use flash cards and paste examples of words into her notebook.
   **c.** focus on important words that she needs to understand.
   **d.** have the student tap out the syllables of words that she knows really well.

**25.** A teacher gives the struggling writers in the class the following worksheet:

*I learned a lot about _____.*
*I learned that _____*
*_____.*
*I also learned that _____*
*_____. The*
*most interesting thing I learned was _____*
*_____.*

What strategy is the teacher using?
**a.** sentence combining
**b.** framed paragraph
**c.** paragraph hamburger
**d.** writing conferences

**26.** The purposes of framed paragraphs are all of the following EXCEPT which one?
**a.** The frame provides a framework for writing strong paragraphs.
**b.** The frame guides students by providing the transitional phrases for sentences.
**c.** The frame can incorporate various sentence types (e.g., long and short, simple and complex).
**d.** The process encourages interesting word choices and transition words.

**27.** A third-grade teacher wants the students in the class to organize their ideas into structured and cohesive paragraphs. What strategy could the teacher use?
**a.** sentence combining
**b.** framed paragraph
**c.** paragraph hamburger
**d.** writing conferences

**28.** A teacher gives the students in the class the following worksheet:

Name: _____     Story Title: _____

| Beginning: | Middle: | End: |
|---|---|---|
| _____ | _____ | _____ |
| _____ | _____ | _____ |
| _____ | _____ | _____ |
| _____ | _____ | _____ |
|  |  |  |

What type of graphic organizer is the teacher using?
**a.** cause and effect
**b.** framed paragraph
**c.** Venn diagram
**d.** story map

**29.** A teacher gives the students several questions to think about during writing:

*Have I used complete sentences?*
*Are my spelling, capitalization, and punctuation correct?*
*Have I marked corrections that I need?*

What part of the writing process are the students working on?
**a.** prewriting
**b.** drafting
**c.** revising
**d.** editing

**30.** In what order does the writing process take place?
  **a.** publishing, editing, revising, drafting, prewriting
  **b.** drafting, prewriting, editing, revising, publishing
  **c.** prewriting, drafting, revising, editing, publishing
  **d.** prewriting, drafting, editing, revising, publishing

**31.** A kindergarten teacher is concerned about a student in the class because the young girl is not progressing with reading and writing at the same rate as the rest of the class. The student and the teacher practice sight words, and the next day the young girl does not remember them. What can the teacher do to help her?
  **a.** Hold off practicing sight words for a little while and instead focus on incorporating reading and writing into everyday fun activities.
  **b.** Continue to practice the same sight words until she knows them.
  **c.** Give the student more time to practice the sight words in class.
  **d.** Give the student homework so she can reinforce the same words learned in class.

**32.** A teacher has several students who cannot organize their writing, and they become extremely frustrated when asked to write a three-paragraph essay. What can the teacher use to help these students?
  **a.** Allow students to draw pictures instead.
  **b.** Allow students to write the best way they can.
  **c.** Use computers to have them write.
  **d.** Use graphic organizers.

**33.** By kindergarten most students will be able to do all of the following EXCEPT
  **a.** sound like they are reading when pretending to read.
  **b.** enjoy being read to and retell simple stories.
  **c.** use descriptive language to write.
  **d.** recognize letters and letter–sound matches.

**34.** What is the purpose of cooperative learning?
  **a.** Cooperative learning involves more than students working together; it requires teachers to structure cooperative interdependence among the students.
  **b.** Cooperative learning is the same as ability grouping, where a teacher divides up the class in order to instruct students with similar skills.
  **c.** Cooperative learning is having students sit side by side at the same table to talk while they complete individual assignments.
  **d.** Cooperative learning is assigning a task to a group in which one student does the work and the others get equal credit.

**35.** What is this image showing?

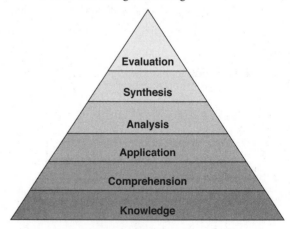

  **a.** taxonomy of learning
  **b.** Structure of Observed Learning Outcomes (SOLO) taxonomy
  **c.** Bloom's taxonomy of learning
  **d.** ten-level taxonomy of data

**36.** What level of questions, according to Bloom's taxonomy, is shown in the following?

*Name three states of water in the water cycle.*
*How many times did you visit the ocean station?*
*What is the definition of transpiration?*

  **a.** knowledge
  **b.** comprehension
  **c.** analysis
  **d.** evaluation

**37.** What level of questions, according to Bloom's taxonomy, is shown in the following?

*What are the advantages and disadvantages of cloud seeding?*
*What part do humans play in the water cycle?*

  **a.** knowledge
  **b.** comprehension
  **c.** analysis
  **d.** evaluation

**38.** What level of questions, according to Bloom's taxonomy, is shown in the following?

*Create a story about what you experienced during your journey.*
*If the average temperature of the earth increased by five degrees Celsius, where might activity in the water cycle change, and why?*

  **a.** knowledge
  **b.** comprehension
  **c.** analysis
  **d.** evaluation

# Mathematics

**39.** Bobby has $\frac{3}{4}$ lb. of dog food. He needs to feed six dogs equally. How much will each dog be given? What is this question asking Bobby to do?
  **a.** Multiply three-fourths by 0.6
  **b.** Divide three-fourths by 6
  **c.** Divide three-fourths into 8
  **d.** Multiply three-fourths by 8

**40.** The teacher wants the students to find the tenth power of 5. What response should the teacher expect from the students?
  **a.** 9,765,625
  **b.** 100,000
  **c.** 50
  **d.** none of the above

**41.** Which visual model does not show the quotient of fractions and whole numbers?
  **a.** fraction bar
  **b.** number line
  **c.** area models
  **d.** pie chart

**42.** The teacher is reviewing equivalent fractions. The teacher asks students to identify equivalent fractions. Which fractions are equivalent?
  **a.** $\frac{2}{3}, \frac{4}{6}, \frac{6}{9}$
  **b.** $\frac{3}{9}, \frac{3}{4}$
  **c.** $\frac{10}{2}, \frac{1}{10}$
  **d.** $\frac{16}{2}, 16\frac{2}{3}$

**43.** The teacher asks students to turn $3\frac{4}{5}$ into $\frac{19}{5}$. What is the teacher asking students to do?
  **a.** reduce fractions
  **b.** convert fractions
  **c.** add fractions
  **d.** subtract fractions

**44.** Kirby has $4\frac{1}{3}$ cups of candy. He eats $\frac{2}{3}$ cups in a serving. How many servings does Kirby eat before finishing all the candy?

What is the question asking students to do?
   **a.** This question is really asking how many $\frac{2}{3}$'s are in $\frac{13}{3}$; in other words, to divide $\frac{13}{3}$ by $\frac{2}{3}$, or $6\frac{1}{2}$.
   **b.** This question is asking how much candy Kirby ate in all.
   **c.** This question is asking how much candy Kirby ate in a single serving.
   **d.** none of the above

**45.** The teacher asks students to write an equation using this information: Aliana has 7 video games. Her cousin has 6 times as many video games. How many video games does her cousin have?
   **a.** $7 + 6 = 13$
   **b.** 1
   **c.** $7 \times 6 = 42$
   **d.** 76

**46.** Mr. Pace will randomly select a student in his fifth-grade class to carry the lunch crate. There are 20 students in his class. There are 13 boys and 7 girls. Mr. Pace could use this as a teachable moment to
   **a.** teach only fractions.
   **b.** teach only probability.
   **c.** teach fractions and probability.
   **d.** teach reducing fractions.

**47.** A fifth-grade teacher put this on the board:

Fill in the missing cell.

| Number of octopuses | 1 | 2 | 3 | 4 |
|---|---|---|---|---|
| Number of legs | 8 | 16 | ? | 32 |

Antwain answered 11. What did he do wrong?
   **a.** He added.
   **b.** He subtracted.
   **c.** He guessed.
   **d.** He divided.

**48.** A fifth-grade teacher puts the following problem on the board: Which number rounds to 7,000 when rounded to the nearest hundred?
   **a.** 6,500
   **b.** 6,990
   **c.** 6,899
   **d.** 6,849

**49.** A third-grade teacher asks her class to find the product of $5 \times 7$ and then check it using the inverse operation. How would this be shown?
   **a.** $7 \times 5 = 35$
   **b.** $35 \div 7 = 5$
   **c.** $5 \div 7 = 35$
   **d.** $35 \div 5 = 5$

**50.** A second-grade teacher gives this problem: $24 + 8$. Helen answered 104. What did she do wrong?
   **a.** She subtracted.
   **b.** She didn't line up the place values when she added.
   **c.** She added.
   **d.** She divided.

**51.** A sixth-grade teacher puts the following problem on the board: What are the lengths of the sides of a square with an area of 36 square feet?
   **a.** 144 feet
   **b.** 9 feet
   **c.** 6 feet
   **d.** 24 feet

**52.** A second-grade teacher asks her class to write 7,041 in expanded form. A student then says the answer is: $700 + 40 + 1$. What did she do wrong?
   **a.** She wrote it in standard form.
   **b.** She wrote it in word form.
   **c.** She wrote the wrong value for the digit 7.
   **d.** She wrote the wrong value for the digit 4.

**53.** A fifth-grade teacher puts this problem on the board:

*I have 6 autobiographies, 35 nonfiction, 10 biographies, and 9 fantasy books. I display my books equally in 3 cases. Which shows how I will find the number of books to put in each case?*

**a.** $3 \times 60$

**b.** $60 \div 6$

**c.** $60 \div 3$

**d.** $60 \div 2$

**54.** Which unit of measure is best for measuring the amount of water in an eyedropper?

**a.** liter

**b.** meter

**c.** milliliter

**d.** millimeter

**55.** A fifth-grade teacher gives the class the following problem: $34 \div 3 + 7 - 5$. What step should be done first?

**a.** 34

**b.** $34 \div 3$

**c.** $3 + 7$

**d.** $7 - 5$

**56.** A fifth-grade teacher puts the following problem on the board:

*Write in standard form: 3 thousands + 7 tens + 6 ones.*

A student answers 376. What did the student do wrong?

**a.** He or she forgot the hundreds place.

**b.** He or she mixed up the tens and ones digits.

**c.** He or she forgot a comma.

**d.** He or she switched the values for the thousands and hundreds place.

**57.** A fourth-grade teacher wants to show that $\frac{1}{5}$ is greater than $\frac{1}{10}$. How should this be done?

**a.** Divide them

**b.** Divide a piece of paper into fifths, then fold it in half, showing tenths

**c.** Add them

**d.** Subtract them

**58.** A fifth-grade teacher is having difficulty getting students to understand how to find the distance between ordered pairs $(x, y)$ on the board. How could the teacher better demonstrate this?

**a.** Use a pointer

**b.** Use a highlighter

**c.** Create a coordinate plane out of floor tiles and use students as manipulatives

**d.** Use an overhead projector

**59.** A second-grade teacher is going to teach about fractions in class. What can she use to introduce this topic?

**a.** pizza pie

**b.** ice cream

**c.** multiplication facts

**d.** patterns

**60.** A third-grade teacher wants to teach about perpendicular lines. Which real-world example would be best?

**a.** an intersection

**b.** cars

**c.** bicycles

**d.** railroad tracks

## Science

**61.** Thermal expansion happens when volume is increased because temperature rises. What device could the teacher use to create a system where thermal expansion occurs?
a. beaker with water in a refrigerator
b. beaker with water at room temperature
c. beaker with water on a hot plate
d. an empty beaker at room temperature

**62.** Using microscopes to observe microorganisms instead of a magnifying lens addresses which standard for third-grade students?
a. teaching methods
b. scientific data
c. materials
d. model building and forecasting

**63.** A fourth-grade teacher instructs her students to use a Punnett square to predict the gene combinations, or inherited traits, of pea plants based on the research performed by Gregor Mendel. What is the best choice that describes the teacher's method of instruction?
a. guided discovery
b. problem solving
c. personal or social perspective
d. history and nature of science

**64.** Gases are well separated with no spatial arrangement. Gases move freely at very high speeds. What category of science would the study of gases fit in?
a. physical science
b. life science
c. health
d. space science

**65.** Two students are working in pairs on an experiment where they have to observe and describe the physical change from liquid water to ice. Student A says the process is called freezing. Student B says the process is called condensing. Which student should the teacher offer extra assistance to?
a. Student A
b. Student B
c. Both students
d. Neither student

**66.** A second-grade teacher instructs her students to ask one another's age and make a bar chart of their distribution. This instructs in which science process objective?
a. defining variables
b. recording data
c. identifying a problem
d. creating models

**67.** Before beginning a geography lesson, a second-grade teacher asks the students to place a pin on their street on the state map. What instructional method is the teacher using to engage the students?
a. constructing ideas and explanations
b. personal perspective of science
c. language and communication
d. problem solving

**68.** A teacher instructs the students to use a given word bank of scientific processes and materials and divide it into one of two categories: life science or physical science. What teaching method is being used?
a. motions and forces
b. science and inquiry
c. management of ideas and information
d. form and function

**69.** A fifth-grade teacher asks the students create a model of the solar system using their textbook and the Internet as a reference. What instructional method is being used?
   **a.** investigation
   **b.** laboratory approach
   **c.** direct instruction
   **d.** games

**70.** During what unit would the students learn about the environment an organism thrives in?
   **a.** health
   **b.** physical science
   **c.** earth science
   **d.** life science

**71.** A fifth-grade science teacher is presenting a lesson on chemical changes. If the student understands the process, which choice will he or she choose?
   **a.** molding clay
   **b.** crumpling a sheet of paper
   **c.** freezing water
   **d.** burning wood

## Social Studies

**72.** During a geography lesson, the teacher asks students to put a peg on the state where the Iroquois lived. Which state should the students put the peg on?
   **a.** California
   **b.** New York
   **c.** Arizona
   **d.** Seattle

**73.** The teacher wants students to understand the benefits of working together. The teacher asks the students why cooperation is important for the survival of the Eskimos. Which is the best reason for the Eskimos cooperating?
   **a.** Eskimos had to make use of everything to survive.
   **b.** Eskimos relied on the best hunters for food.
   **c.** Eskimos lived in harmony with the environment.
   **d.** all of the above

**74.** The fifth-grade teacher probes for student understanding: How did specialization come about? Which student response lets the teacher know that students understand what specialization means?
   **a.** A surplus of food meant not everyone needed to farm.
   **b.** A surplus of food meant everyone needed to farm.
   **c.** When fewer people were farming, more food was produced.
   **d.** When more people were needed to farm, fewer people learned the technique of farming.

**75.** Which lesson and discipline should be taught at the same time as latitude and longitude to aid students in understanding their purpose and usefulness?
   **a.** diagramming sentences, English
   **b.** scientific method, science
   **c.** scale, social studies
   **d.** coordinate planes, math

**76.** Which imaginary line divides the earth into eastern and western hemispheres?
   **a.** prime meridian
   **b.** international date line
   **c.** equator
   **d.** Antarctic circle

**77.** Which colony did not send representatives to the first Continental Congress meeting?
   **a.** New York
   **b.** Concord
   **c.** Boston
   **d.** Georgia

**78.** Which was the last English colony settled? What level of cognitive thought is this question?
   **a.** application
   **b.** knowledge
   **c.** evaluation
   **d.** creation

**79.** The teacher wants students to map the place of departure for the Puritans and where they settled in the New World. A student is chosen to report on the outcome of the map to the class. Which level of Bloom's taxonomy is this?
   **a.** applying
   **b.** understanding
   **c.** analyzing
   **d.** evaluating

**80.** At the end of the lesson, the teacher asks students: *What was the goal of the Continental Congress meeting in 1774?* Which answer would let the teacher know the depth of students' understanding of the meeting of the Continental Congress?
   **a.** to persuade King George to change the tax laws
   **b.** to prepare for war
   **c.** to pick George Washington as leader
   **d.** to seize a gunpowder supply at Concord

**81.** Which is a draft of a proposed law?
   **a.** bill
   **b.** article
   **c.** guideline
   **d.** treaty

**82.** What was/were the primary reason(s) for the Revolutionary War? If the students understand what the word *primary* means, what should they answer?
   **a.** English law prohibited slavery in free states to free men.
   **b.** The colonists were concerned their economy and way of life would be disrupted.
   **c.** The colonists felt that taxes were too high and burdensome.
   **d.** all of the above

## Arts and Physical Education

**83.** During a lesson on nutrition, the teacher tells the students that calcium, which is an important mineral, is commonly found in milk. The teacher then informs the students that the calcium ingested by drinking milk can aid in building bones, teeth, and maintaining bone strength. Which is the theme of this lesson?
   **a.** locomotor patterns
   **b.** healthy lifestyles
   **c.** exercise
   **d.** physical fitness

**84.** A fourth-grade teacher instructs the students to mix two primary colors to create orange for their painting assignment. If the students understand the task, which primary colors will they choose?
   **a.** yellow and blue
   **b.** red and green
   **c.** red and yellow
   **d.** blue and red

**85.** The student wants to draw two shapes, each with only two lines of symmetry. The student decides to draw a square and a diamond. Is the student making a mistake? If so, where?

    **a.** Yes, a diamond does not have two lines of symmetry.

    **b.** Yes, a diamond has two lines of symmetry.

    **c.** Yes, a square has four lines of symmetry, not two.

    **d.** No, the student chose correctly.

**86.** The student wants to make a presentation using secondary colors. What colors can the student choose?

    **a.** green and orange

    **b.** blue and orange

    **c.** yellow and green

    **d.** red and orange

**87.** Identify the following symbol:

    **a.** rest

    **b.** treble clef

    **c.** bass clef

    **d.** half note

**88.** The students are reading their music sheets. They see an eighth note in $\frac{4}{4}$ time. How long will they hold the note for?

    **a.** $\frac{1}{4}$ beat

    **b.** $\frac{1}{3}$ beat

    **c.** $\frac{1}{2}$ beat

    **d.** one beat

**89.** In the time signature, what does the bottom number represent?

    **a.** how many notes per minute

    **b.** the type of note

    **c.** what note receives one beat

    **d.** how many beats per measure

**90.** Carbohydrates are important because they

    **a.** make you feel good.

    **b.** store your energy.

    **c.** give you most of your energy.

    **d.** help you think.

**91.** Why is dietary fiber important for your body? Fiber helps your body _____ the removal of water from the _____.

    **a.** slow down; large intestine

    **b.** speed up; large intestine

    **c.** slow down; small intestine

    **d.** speed up; small intestine

**92.** When you eat more simple carbohydrates than you need, your body then turns the extra carbohydrates into

    **a.** fat.

    **b.** sugar.

    **c.** muscle.

    **d.** bone.

**93.** The teacher asks students to use secondary colors in their spring visual flower display. What colors can the students choose?

    **a.** green and purple

    **b.** red and orange

    **c.** red and yellow

    **d.** green and blue

## General

**94.** A teacher asked her fourth-grade class,

"Sammy is giving out pencils at his party. He is having 22 children at his party, and each child will receive one pencil. Pencils are sold in packs of five. How many packs should Sammy buy?"

What level of Bloom's taxonomy is the teacher using?
**a.** application
**b.** comprehension
**c.** knowledge
**d.** analysis

**95.** Which of the following is not a learning style?
**a.** kinesthetic
**b.** visual
**c.** auditory
**d.** motivational

**96.** Mrs. Howell will randomly select a student in Angela's class to clean the board. There are 23 students in the class. What is the probability Mrs. Howell will choose Angela?
**a.** 1 out of 22
**b.** 22 out of 23
**c.** 1 out of 23
**d.** 23 out of 1

**97.** Why is student-centered instruction preferred?
**a.** It focuses on students and teachers interacting equally.
**b.** It stresses cooperative learning.
**c.** It involves learning by doing.
**d.** It best addresses Common Core state standards.

**98.** Which of the following is a summative assessment?
**a.** project learning
**b.** oral reports
**c.** report card grades
**d.** teacher observation

**99.** A fourth-grade teacher puts the following problem on the board:

*Write a number that rounds to 600 when rounded to the nearest hundred.*
**a.** 650
**b.** 651
**c.** 549
**d.** 551

**100.** Kendall has 8 fiction, 15 nonfiction, and 7 biography books. He displays his books equally in two cases. Which calculation shows how he found the number of books to put in each case?
**a.** $2 \times 16$
**b.** $16 \div 2$
**c.** $2 \times 30$
**d.** $30 \div 2$

**101.** A fifth-grade teacher wants to teach about probability. Which manipulative would provide the least number of outcomes?
**a.** coin
**b.** die
**c.** three-section spinner
**d.** deck of cards

**102.** A fifth-grade teacher asks students to summarize the events leading up to the Missouri Compromise. Which is the best way for the students to present their information?
**a.** bar graph
**b.** line graph
**c.** *x–y* plot
**d.** pie chart

**103.** A third-grade class is getting ready to read about the Great Compromise. The teacher contrives a situation where the students learn what it means to compromise by having experienced it. Which learning style is the teacher addressing?
  **a.** kinesthetic learners
  **b.** role playing
  **c.** visual learners
  **d.** auditory learners

**104.** What type of learners would rather listen to things being explained than read about them?
  **a.** kinesthetic learners
  **b.** tactile learners
  **c.** visual learners
  **d.** auditory learners

**105.** A teacher turns in a lesson plan that gives a description of the students along with the instructional objectives, ways to activate learning, instructional strategies, and materials. What is the teacher demonstrating?
  **a.** knowledge of a range of resources
  **b.** ability to design coherent instruction
  **c.** an established environment of respect and rapport
  **d.** an established culture for learning

**106.** What is the best way to demonstrate knowledge of subject matter and pedagogy?
  **a.** Develop lessons based on best practice.
  **b.** Set goals that are achievable and age appropriate.
  **c.** Use authentic real-world assessments.
  **d.** Appreciate each child's contribution.

**107.** After each lesson, a third-grade teacher evaluates her approach to teaching and assesses learning. What is the teacher demonstrating?
  **a.** reflecting on teaching practice
  **b.** demonstrating professionalism
  **c.** professional growth and development
  **d.** developing lessons based on best practice

**108.** The teachers send home welcome letters at the start of each unit. What would be the best reason for informing parents of what the students will be learning in class?
  **a.** to establish a partnership with families
  **b.** to keep parents informed about the instructional program
  **c.** to build a sense of community
  **d.** all of the above

**109.** The social studies teacher asks students their opinion of the Emancipation Proclamation:

*Now, therefore I, Abraham Lincoln, President of the United States, by virtue of the power in me vested as Commander-in-Chief, of the Army and Navy of the United States in time of actual armed rebellion against the authority and government of the United States, and as a fit and necessary war measure for suppressing said rebellion, do, on this first day of January, in the year of our Lord one thousand eight hundred and sixty-three, and in accordance with my purpose so to do publicly proclaimed for the full period of one hundred days, from the day first above mentioned, order and designate as the States and parts of States wherein the people thereof respectively, are this day in rebellion against the United States, the following, to wit: Arkansas, Texas, Louisiana (except the Parishes of St. Bernard, Plaquemines, Jefferson, St. John, St. Charles, St. James Ascension, Assumption, Terrebonne, Lafourche, St. Mary, St. Martin, and Orleans, including the City of New Orleans), Mississippi, Alabama, Florida, Georgia, South Carolina, North Carolina, and Virginia (except the forty-eight counties designated as West Virginia, and also the counties of Berkley, Accomac, Northampton, Elizabeth City, York, Princess Ann, and Norfolk, including the cities of Norfolk and Portsmouth), and which excepted parts, are for the present, left precisely as if this proclamation were not issued.*

Which standard is being addressed by the teacher?

**a.** Key ideas and details: Quote accurately from a text when explaining what the text says explicitly and when drawing inferences from the text.
**b.** Craft and structure: Determine meaning of words and phrases as they are used in the text.
**c.** Integration of knowledge and ideas: Integrate information from several texts.
**d.** Range of reading and level of text complexity: By end of year students will read and comprehend informational text.

**110.** The teacher asks students questions. Which question arouses low-order thinking?
**a.** What do you remember about the Battle of the Bulge?
**b.** How would you differentiate between the Union and the Confederate armies?
**c.** How could you develop the plot of the story?
**d.** How can you describe the author's purpose?

# Answers and Explanations

## *Reading and Language Arts*

**1. a.** Several words that begin with the same letter or sound are repeated in the sentence. Choice **b** is incorrect because there are no words that describe a sound. Choice **c** is incorrect because the line is not comparing two things using *like* or *as*. Choice **d** is incorrect because the line is not comparing two unlike things.

**2. a.** The text includes the causes for Elianna's sunburn (e.g., a full day outdoors and a lack of sunscreen), which the students must discern to answer the question. Choice **b** is incorrect because the text is properly sequenced. Choice **c** is incorrect because the students are not comparing and contrasting varying sets of information. Choice **d** is incorrect because the passage is not quite long enough to expand upon a main idea and details; it includes only the essential information to determine cause and effect.

**3. d.** Students need to understand that *retrieving* has a similar meaning to other words. Choice **a** is incorrect because we are not asking students to find the definition of the word. Choice **b** is incorrect because the students do not have to figure out the figure of speech in the question. Choice **c** is incorrect because students are not asked to understand language conventions.

**4. a.** Using this strategy will allow the teacher to check students' onset–rime awareness, which allows the teacher to determine if they are able to rhyme. Choices **b** and **c** are incorrect because these strategies allow the teacher to determine whether the students can hear and count syllables. Choice **d** is incorrect because that strategy allows the teacher to assess phonemic awareness.

**5. c.** This strategy allows the teacher to teach letter–sound relationships, not letter recognition. Choices **a**, **b**, and **d** are all strategies that would help in letter recognition.

**6. d.** To help students understand the word *transformation*, the teacher must build and activate students' background knowledge of the word. Choice **a** is incorrect because understanding prediction will not help the students understand the word. Choice **b** is incorrect because visualizing the word will not help students understand the word. Choice **c** is incorrect because questioning will not help to understand the word.

**7. c.** The teacher is asking the students to compose a nonfiction text with information that is factual. Choice **a** is incorrect because a personal narrative is a story about something that has happened in the student's life. Choice **b** is incorrect because the students are not asked to write a persuasive writing piece. Choice **d** is incorrect because the teacher is not asking the students to write a journal entry.

**8. c.** Giving a midterm test is a type of summative assessment and not a formative assessment. Choices **a**, **b**, and **d** are all types of formative assessments.

**9. c.** A teacher cannot test a student's ability to read for pleasure. Choices **a**, **b**, and **d** are incorrect because all can be tested using summative assessments.

**10. d.** Giving students a word bank and brainstorming with them allows students to see sight words and use them. Choice **a** is incorrect because these activities do not build vocabulary. Choice **b** is incorrect because they do not help with ideas. Choice **c** is incorrect because they do not help with writing.

**11. d.** It is best not to teach in isolation but in context with everyday lessons. Choice **a** is incorrect because students will not retain grammar rules without teaching in context. Choice **b** is incorrect because just making them do writing assignments will not help with grammar. Choice **c** is incorrect because a teacher can give clear examples and explanations, but they will not help without learning in context.

**12. c.** When students can see the text, this allows them to read along with the teacher, who is modeling fluency. Choice **a** is incorrect because it does not allow them to read at home if they do not have the books. Choice **b** is incorrect because having a "big book" does not mean that there will be a lot of information in it. Choice **d** is incorrect because when reading a "big book" the teacher does not use shared writing.

**13. b.** The writing process involves prewriting, drafting, editing, and revising. Choice **a** is incorrect because it is not a process of reading. Choice **c** is incorrect because it does not show a process of listening. Choice **d** is incorrect because it does not show a process of speaking.

**14. d.** Cooperative work allows students to collaborate, think, and problem solve together as a group. Choices **a**, **b**, and **c** are incorrect because those are not the purposes of cooperative work.

**15. b.** Historical fiction books are works of fiction except for the time period, the historical events, and the setting. Choices **a**, **c**, and **d** are incorrect because those are not works that are true to a historical time period.

**16. c.** The purpose of modifying students' work is not to find their weaknesses, but to have them feel accomplished in the same work the other students are doing. Choices **a**, **b**, and **d** are all questions teachers should ask themselves when thinking about modifying lessons.

**17. a.** The school is looking at summative assessments to help strengthen curriculum and instruction in the school. Choice **b** is incorrect because formative assessments are not formal assessments. Choice **c** is incorrect because state and local tests are not alternative assessments. Choice **d** is incorrect because they are not interim assessments.

**18. b.** The organizer is a semantic map that shows a visual representation of knowledge using words. Choice **a** is incorrect because the organizer is not a story map. Choice **c** is incorrect because it is not a K-W-L chart. Choice **d** is incorrect because it is not a T-chart.

**19. a.** Having students use academic language and work together collaboratively addresses this standard. Choices **b**, **c**, and **d** are incorrect because they do not address what is going to happen in the classroom.

**20. b.** A teacher should not water down the curriculum for ELLs in the classroom; teachers have to make it more comprehensible for them. Choices **a**, **c**, and **d** are examples of modifications a teacher can use with the ELLs in the classroom.

**21. a.** The students have to use the glossaries on their own. Choices **b**, **c**, and **d** are incorrect because these are examples of teacher-directed, not student-directed, learning for vocabulary instruction.

**22. b.** When students can hear phonemes in words, they have phonemic awareness. Choice **a** is incorrect because it is an example of syllabic awareness. Choice **c** is incorrect because it is onset–rime awareness. Choice **d** is incorrect because it is the ability to listen for vocabulary.

**23. d.** The use of Elkonin boxes is not to listen to vocabulary. Choices **a**, **b**, and **c** are examples of why a teacher would use Elkonin boxes.

**24. a.** Before a teacher can continue working with the student, the young girl needs to be able to make letters. Choices **b**, **c**, and **d** are incorrect because she cannot continue working on these until she can use and hold a pencil properly.

**25. b.** The example is a framed paragraph to help struggling writers. Choices **a**, **c**, and **d** are all incorrect.

**26. d.** A framed paragraph does not help struggling writers with word choices or transition words. Choices **a**, **b**, and **c** are examples of the purposes of a framed paragraph.

**27. c.** Paragraph hamburger is a means of organizing paragraphs that students can relate to. Choice **a** is incorrect because the question focuses on organizing paragraphs, not sentence combining. Choice **b** is incorrect because the students are trying to assemble and organize complete paragraphs. Choice **d** is incorrect because conferences come after a completed writing assignment.

**28. d.** The organizer shows an example of a story map to help students organize the beginning, middle, and end of a story. Choices **a**, **b**, and **c** are incorrect.

**29. d.** When students have reached the editing part of the writing process, they have to think about correcting sentences, capitalization, punctuation, and other grammatical errors. Choices **a**, **b**, and **c** are incorrect because they are not questions to ask when a student is at the prewriting, drafting, or revising phase of the writing process.

**30. c.** This is the order of the writing process. Choices **a**, **b**, and **d** are incorrect because they do not follow the writing process.

**31. a.** The student is not developmentally ready, so it is important that the teacher continue to incorporate other activities that are fun but can reinforce reading and writing. Choices **b**, **c**, and **d** are incorrect because they can frustrate the student and turn her off to learning.

**32. d.** A teacher can give students a graphic organizer to help them organize their ideas without having them feel frustrated while writing. Choice **a** is incorrect because they should also be held accountable for writing. Choice **b** is incorrect because they will continue to get frustrated. Choice **c** is incorrect because they still need to feel like their writing is organized before getting on the computer to write.

**33. c.** Most students will not be developmentally able to use descriptive language to write. Choices **a**, **b**, and **d** are correct because most students will be able to do these by the time they are in kindergarten.

**34. a.** Cooperative learning is a structured lesson that allows all students to cooperate together. Choice **b** is incorrect because the teacher is not grouping students by ability. Choice **c** is incorrect because the students are not sitting near each other and just talking. Choice **d** is incorrect because it does not involve one student doing all the work.

**35. c.** It is an example of Bloom's taxonomy of learning. Choices **a**, **b**, and **d** are incorrect because they are not represented by the image.

**36. a.** The questions determine the students' knowledge of factual information. Choice **b** is incorrect because the questions do not determine the students' understanding of the subject. Choice **c** is incorrect because they do not require students to separate their knowledge into its components and apply it to new situations. Choice **d** is incorrect because they do not allow the students to make judgments and opinions.

**37. d.** The questions allow the students to make judgments and opinions. Choice **a** is incorrect because they do not determine the students' knowledge of factual information. Choice **b** is incorrect because they do not determine the students' understanding of the subject. Choice **c** is incorrect because they do not require students to separate their knowledge into its components and apply it to new situations.

**38. c.** The questions require students to separate their knowledge into its components and apply it to new situations. Choice **a** is incorrect because the questions do not determine the students' knowledge of factual information. Choice **b** is incorrect because they do not determine the students' understanding of the subject. Choice **d** is incorrect because they do not allow the students to make judgments and opinions.

## Mathematics

**39. b.** Three-fourths needs to be divided by 6 to get $\frac{1}{8}$. Each dog will get $\frac{1}{8}$ lb. of dog food Choice **a** is incorrect because multiplication is not the correct operation for this problem. Choice **c** is incorrect because there are 6 dogs, not 8. Choice **d** is incorrect because multiplication is not the correct operation for this problem.

**40. a.** The tenth power of 5 is $5^{10}$, which is $5 \times 5 \times 5 \times 5 \times 5 \times 5 \times 5 \times 5 \times 5 \times 5 = 9,765,625$. Choice **b** is incorrect because it is the fifth power of ten, which is $10 \times 10 \times 10 \times 10 \times 10 = 100,000$. Choice **c** is incorrect because it is $10 \times 5 = 50$.

**41. b.** A number line only shows numbers in a designated sequence. Choices **a**, **c**, and **d** are incorrect because fraction bars, area models, and pie charts all visually display the quotients of fractions and whole numbers in some form.

**42. a.** All three of these fractions are equivalent, as both $\frac{6}{9}$ and $\frac{4}{6}$ can be reduced to $\frac{2}{3}$. Choice **b** is incorrect because $\frac{3}{9}$ can be reduced to $\frac{1}{3}$, but $\frac{3}{4}$ is not equivalent to either. Choice **c** is incorrect because $\frac{10}{2}$ can be reduced to 5, which is not equivalent to $\frac{1}{10}$. Choice **d** is incorrect because $\frac{16}{2}$ can be reduced to 8, which is not equivalent to $16\frac{2}{3}$.

**43. b.** The teacher is asking the students to convert $3\frac{4}{5}$, which is a mixed number, into its improper fraction equivalent, $\frac{19}{5}$. Choice **a** is incorrect because $3\frac{4}{5}$ cannot be reduced. Choice **c** is incorrect because there is no second fraction to add. Choice **d** is incorrect because there is no second fraction to subtract.

**44. a.** The question is asking students to figure out how many $\frac{2}{3}$-cup servings it took Kirby to eat all $4\frac{1}{3}$ cups of candy. The answer is achieved by dividing $4\frac{1}{3}$ (or $\frac{13}{3}$) by $\frac{2}{3}$ to get $6\frac{1}{2}$. Choice **b** is incorrect because it is already stated that Kirby has $4\frac{1}{3}$ cups of candy in all. Choice **c** is incorrect because it is already stated that Kirby eats $\frac{2}{3}$-cup servings.

**45. c.** Since Aliana's cousin has 6 times as many games as Aliana, the correct solution for this problem is to multiply the number of Aliana's video games by 6. Choice **a** is incorrect because it simply adds 7 and 6 to get 13. Choice **b** is incorrect because nowhere does it state that Aliana or her cousin had one game. Choice **d** is incorrect because it simply puts the 7 and the 6 together to form 76.

**46. c.** With the information at hand, Mr. Pace could demonstrate how to make fractions based on the number of boys and girls in the class out of a total of 20 students; he could then show the varying probabilities of boys versus girls carrying the lunch crate. Choice **a** is incorrect because there is an opportunity to teach probability. Choice **b** is incorrect because there is an opportunity to teach fractional representation. Choice **d** is incorrect because $\frac{7}{20}$ and $\frac{13}{20}$ are not opportunities to teach reducing fractions.

**47. c.** The student followed no logical pattern in selecting his answer. Choices **a**, **b**, and **d** imply that the student followed some type of logical pattern in selecting his (incorrect) answer.

**48. b.** This choice is the closest to 7,000 when rounded up to the nearest hundred. Choice **a** is incorrect because it is already an evenly rounded number. Choice **c** is incorrect because it would be 6,900 when rounded to the nearest hundred. Choice **d** is incorrect because it would be 6,800 when rounded to the nearest hundred.

**49. b.** The inverse operation of multiplication is division, and to properly check this problem requires dividing the product (35) by one of the multiples (7) to arrive at 5. Choice **a** is incorrect because it does not use the inverse operation to check the problem. Choices **c** and **d** are incorrect because the equations themselves are incorrect despite using the correct inverse operation.

**50. b.** The student placed the 8 in the tens column when adding, thus adding the 2 and the 8 and retaining the 4 to arrive at 104. Choice **a** is incorrect because if the student subtracted 8 from 24 she would have arrived at 16. Choice **c** is incorrect because if the student added 24 and 8 she would have arrived at the correct answer, 32. Choice **d** is incorrect because if the student divided 24 by 8 she would have arrived at 3.

**51. c.** Since area equals length times width, and the sides of a square are equal in length, this problem is solved with the equation $x \times x = 36$, or $x^2 = 36$. The square root of 36 is 6. Choice **a** is incorrect because it is implausible that the length of one side would be greater than the total area. Choice **b** is incorrect because a square with sides of 9 feet would have an area of 81 square feet. Choice **d** is incorrect because a square with sides of 24 feet would have an area of 576 feet.

**52. c.** The student identified the 7 as belonging to the hundreds rather than thousands place, perhaps confused by the 0 in the hundreds place in the standard form. Choice **a** is incorrect because the student did attempt to write the number in expanded form. Choice **b** is incorrect because the student did not write out the number in word form. Choice **d** is incorrect because the student correctly attributed the 4 to the tens place.

**53. c.** This problem is solved by adding the total number of books (60) and dividing by the total number of cases (3). Choice **a** is incorrect because it multiplies the number of books by the number of cases. Choices **b** and **d** are incorrect because they divide the number of books by the wrong number of cases.

**54. c.** Measuring water requires a unit of volume, and the amount in an eyedropper requires a very small unit; this is the smaller of the two choices that are units of volume. Choice **a** is incorrect because it is too large a unit of volume. Choices **b** and **d** are incorrect because they are units of length.

**55. b.** When following the order of operations, division is done before addition or subtraction. Choice **a** is incorrect because it is not a step. Choices **c** and **d** are incorrect because division is done before addition or subtraction according to the order of operations.

**56. a.** The student neglected to include a 0 in the hundreds place. Choice **b** is incorrect because the student correctly attributed the 7 to the tens place and the 6 to the ones place. Choice **c** is incorrect because, though a comma between the thousands and hundreds place would be necessary in standard form (four digits), the student did not write the standard form correctly (only three digits). Choice **d** is incorrect because the student did not include a value for the thousands place in his or her answer.

**57. d.** By subtracting $\frac{1}{10}$ from $\frac{1}{5}$, the teacher will have to convert $\frac{1}{5}$ to $\frac{2}{10}$, thus showing that $\frac{2}{10} - \frac{1}{10} = \frac{1}{10}$; in other words, $\frac{1}{5}$ is one-tenth larger than $\frac{1}{10}$. Choice **a** is incorrect because dividing the fractions does not demonstrate as easily that $\frac{1}{5}$ is larger than $\frac{1}{10}$. Choice **b** is incorrect because the visual demonstration is less precise in showing that $\frac{1}{5}$ is larger than $\frac{1}{10}$. Choice **c** is incorrect because, while the teacher will have to convert $\frac{1}{5}$ to $\frac{2}{10}$, adding the two fractions does not demonstrate how $\frac{1}{5}$ is one-tenth larger than $\frac{1}{10}$.

**58. c.** If the students are not understanding the distance between the pairs when confined to the board, the best option is to involve them in the demonstration. Choices **a**, **b**, and **d** are incorrect because they do not add a further dimension to the demonstration, keeping it confined to the board (or, in the case of choice **d**, the flat surface of the overhead projection).

**59. a.** The circular shape of the pizza cut into various slices is the clearest visual aid for introducing fractions. Choice **b** is incorrect because it is difficult to represent ice cream fractionally. Choice **c** is incorrect because multiplication facts do not directly relate to the introduction of fractions. Choice **d** is incorrect because patterns are too general and do not ground the students' learning in a visual way.

**60. a.** The intersection of two roads is the clearest visual aid for the introduction of the concept of perpendicularity. Choices **b** and **c** are incorrect because cars and bicycles can move in all sorts of directions and do not ground the students' learning in a visual way. Choice **d** is incorrect because railroad tracks are a real-world example of parallel lines.

### Science

**61. c.** A beaker on a hot plate will generate heat, allowing the water volume to increase and thermal expansion to occur. Choice **a** is incorrect because a beaker with water in a refrigerator would not increase in temperature. Choice **b** is incorrect because a beaker with water at room temperature would not increase in temperature. Choice **d** is incorrect because a liquid is necessary to make the thermal expansion visible.

**62. b.** The scientific data standard consists of choosing the appropriate tools to gather data. Choices **a** and **c** are incorrect because teaching methods and materials would consist of an instructional introduction, not application of the data or instrument. Choice **d** is incorrect because model building and forecasting would be the creation of plans and computer simulations.

**63. d.** The teacher is asking the students to create an investigation based on the history of science, more specifically the research performed by Gregor Mendel with pea plants. Choice **a** is incorrect because the teacher is using a historical model to lead the students toward an answer. Choice **b** is incorrect because the teacher is using a historical model, which is the key term. Choice **c** is incorrect because the data is being looked at through a historical/scientific perspective and not a personal or social perspective.

**64. a.** A gas is a state, or phase, of matter and would be studied in the physical science category. Elements are able to move between the phases (solid, liquid, gas) depending on physical conditions such as temperature. Choices **b**, **c**, and **d** are incorrect.

**65. b.** Student B has confused freezing with condensation. Freezing slows particles down, making them more compacted or solid (ice), whereas condensation is the conversion of a vapor or gas to a liquid. Choices **a**, **c**, and **d** are incorrect.

**66. b.** The students are being instructed to record data and organize it into a graph. Choices **a**, **c**, and **d** are incorrect because there is no variable to define, problem to identify, or model to create.

**67. b.** The teacher is engaging the students by creating a personal perspective of science for them. When the students place a pin on the street they live on, they are now incorporated into the lesson. Choice **a** is incorrect because the placement of the pin does not necessarily involve the construction of an idea or explanation. Choice **c** is incorrect because the placement of the pin does not necessarily involve language and communication skills. Choice **d** is incorrect because the placement of the pin does not necessarily advance problem-solving skills.

**68. c.** The students are being instructed to manage ideas and given information. Choices **a** and **b** are incorrect because the emphasis is on categorization of scientific processes. Choice **d** is incorrect because the teacher does not ask the students to organize the information into a Venn diagram or other specific form.

**69. a.** The students are being instructed to conduct an independent investigation of the solar system. Choices **b** and **c** are incorrect because there is no lab or direct instruction from the teacher. Choice **d** is incorrect because the instructional method would not be considered a game, but research.

**70. d.** Life science consists of the characteristics of organisms, including the environment in which they live. Choice **a** is incorrect because health focuses on the well-being of individuals, placing less emphasis on their external environment. Choice **b** is incorrect because physical science focuses on the properties of matter. Choice **c** is incorrect because earth science consists of the interrelationships of earth and space systems, but not in relation to an organism.

**71. d.** The combustion, or burning, of wood is a chemical change. Once wood is burned, you cannot reverse the process. Choices **a**, **b**, and **c** are incorrect because molding clay, crumpling paper, and freezing water can all be reversed and are considered physical changes.

## Social Studies

**72. b.** The Iroquois lived in New York State. Choice **a** is incorrect because the Iroquois lived on the East Coast, not the West Coast. Choice **c** is incorrect because the Iroquois were not in the Southwest. Choice **d** is incorrect because Seattle was part of the Pacific Northwest and California Intermountain.

**73. b.** Eskimos relied on the best hunters for food in the tundra. Choices **a** and **c** are incorrect because, even though Eskimos did make use of everything to survive and did live in harmony with the environment, the statements do not reflect cooperation.

**74. a.** A surplus of food meant that people could learn other skills. Choice **b** is incorrect because the statement is inaccurate. A surplus is an extra supply; therefore, the extra supply meant that not everyone needed to do the same job. Choice **c** is incorrect because it is inaccurate. Fewer people farming meant less food. Choice **d** is incorrect because more people farming meant that more people learned to farm.

**75. d.** A coordinate plane is formed by a horizontal number line called the $x$-axis and a vertical number line called the $y$-axis. The $x$-axis is equivalent to the equator and its parallel, or latitude lines. The $y$-axis is equivalent to the prime meridian and the other meridians. Choice **a** is incorrect because it is a way of analyzing sentence structure using a visual scheme. A sentence scheme does not necessarily follow a consistent pattern. Choice **b** is incorrect because it has more to do with steps in a process. Choice **c** is incorrect because it has more to do with size and distance.

**76. a.** The prime meridian divides the earth into eastern and western hemispheres. Choice **b** is incorrect because while the international date line is a meridian, it does not divide the earth into eastern and western hemispheres. Choice **c** is incorrect because the equator is an imaginary line that divides the earth into northern and southern hemispheres. Choice **d** is incorrect because the Antarctic circle is a latitude line deep in the southern hemisphere.

**77. d.** Georgia was not present at the first Continental Congress meeting in Philadelphia in 1774. Choice **a** is incorrect because New York was present. Choice **b** is incorrect because Concord is not a colony. It is the town where British soldiers attempted to seize a gunpowder supply. Choice **c** is incorrect because Boston is a settlement in the colony of Massachusetts.

**78. b.** The question requires recall of facts. Choice **a** is incorrect because previous knowledge is not being used in a new way. Choice **c** is incorrect because there is no stand or defense to be made. Choice **d** is incorrect because a new way of thinking is not being established.

**79. b.** The student can explain the ideas and concepts connected to this level. Choice **a** is incorrect because at this level new knowledge is applied in a new way. Choice **c** is incorrect because it requires telling the difference between the parts in relation to the whole. Choice **d** is incorrect because the student can defend a position.

**80. a.** The Continental Congress met in Philadelphia in 1774 for the purpose of trying to persuade King George to change the tax laws. Choice **b** is incorrect because armed conflict did not start until months after the meeting. Choice **c** is incorrect because George Washington was not picked as leader until war was under way. Choice **d** is incorrect because it was the British soldiers who attempted to seize the gunpowder supply at Concord.

**81. a.** A bill is a draft of a proposed law. Choice **b** is incorrect because when Congress created the Constitution, it had seven parts called articles. Choice **c** is incorrect because a guideline is a principle or general rule. Choice **d** is incorrect because a treaty is a formal agreement that has to be ratified by countries.

**82. d.** As in choice **a**, English law did prohibit slavery in free states to free men. As a result, (choice **b**) the colonists were concerned their economy and way of life would be disrupted. The colonists were already paying (choice **c**) taxes that were too high and burdensome.

## Arts and Physical Education

**83. b.** The focus of this lesson is clearly on health and nutrition, and thus developing the habits of a healthy lifestyle. Choice **a** is incorrect because the lesson is not discussing such locomotor patterns as walking or jumping. Choices **c** and **d** are incorrect because the lesson is not discussing exercise or physical fitness routines, but rather nutritional information.

**84. c.** The primary colors of red and yellow, when mixed, create orange. Choice **a** is incorrect because yellow and blue make green. Choice **b** is incorrect because green is not a primary color. Choice **d** is incorrect because blue and red make purple.

**85. c.** A square has four lines of symmetry, in that it can be divided equally lengthwise, widthwise, and corner to corner in both directions. Choice **a** is incorrect because a diamond has two lines of symmetry, in that it can be divided equally lengthwise and widthwise. Choice **b** is not where the student made a mistake. Choice **d** is incorrect because choice **c** is correct.

**86. a.** Green and orange are both secondary colors, derived from mixing primary colors—blue and yellow, and red and yellow, respectively. Choice **b** is incorrect because blue is a primary color. Choice **c** is incorrect because yellow is a primary color. Choice **d** is incorrect because red is a primary color.

**87. c.** The picture is an image of a bass clef. Choice **a** is incorrect because the image is not one of the various types of rests. Choice **b** is incorrect because a treble clef looks like this: 𝄞. Choice **d** is incorrect because a half note looks like this: ♩.

**88. c.** An eighth note (♪) is held for half a beat in $\frac{4}{4}$ time. Choices **a** and **b** are incorrect because $\frac{1}{4}$ beat and $\frac{1}{3}$ beat are not note values in $\frac{4}{4}$ time. Choice **d** is incorrect because a quarter note is held for one beat in $\frac{4}{4}$ time.

**89. c.** The bottom number in the time signature represents what note receives one beat. Choice **d** is incorrect because that is what the top number in a time signature represents. Choices **a** and **b** are incorrect because they have no relation to the time signature.

**90. c.** Carbohydrates are a major energy source. Choice **b** is incorrect because they do not store energy; they provide energy. Choices **a** and **d** are not relevant to carbohydrates.

**91. b.** Dietary fiber is important because it helps speed up the process of removing water from the large intestine. Choices **a** and **c** are both incorrect because dietary fiber does not slow down the removal of water. Choice **d** is incorrect because dietary fiber removes water from the large intestine, not the small intestine.

**92. a.** When you eat more carbohydrates than your body needs, they are then converted into fat. Simple carbohydrates will first turn into glucose (choice **b**) and glycogen, and then are stored in your body. Choices **c** and **d** are incorrect because excess carbohydrates are not turned into muscle or bone.

**93. a.** Green and purple are both secondary colors, derived from mixing primary colors—blue and yellow, and red and blue, respectively. Choice **b** is incorrect because red is a primary color. Choice **c** is incorrect because both red and yellow are primary colors. Choice **d** is incorrect because blue is a primary color.

## General

**94. a.** This question utilizes the application of knowledge to solve a given problem. Choice **b** is incorrect because the question does not require the student to organize or interpret information. Choice **c** is incorrect because the question does not require the student to just recall basic facts or concepts, but rather apply them to the problem. Choice **d** is incorrect because the question does not require the student to identify causes or locate evidence to support a given statement.

**95. d.** Motivational is not a learning style. Kinesthetic learners (choice **a**) prefer learning through experience or doing. Visual learners (choice **b**) prefer to observe the how-to before doing. Auditory learners (choice **c**) prefer hearing.

**96. c.** One student out of the class of 23 will be chosen. Choice **a** is incorrect because there are 23 children in the class. Choice **b** is incorrect because only one student will clean the board, not 22. Choice **d** is incorrect because the numbers are reversed.

**97. a.** Student-centered instruction focuses on students and teachers interacting equally. Choice **b** is incorrect because cooperative learning involves groups of students working together. Choice **c** is incorrect because the statement describes experiential learning. Choice **d** is incorrect because it is irrelevant to student-centered instruction.

**98. c.** Report card grades are a type of summative assessment. Choice **a** is an example of a formative assessment. Choice **b** is a type of formative assessment. Choice **d** is a formative assessment.

**99. d.** The number 551 would round to 600. Choices **a** and **b** are incorrect because they would round to 700. Choice **c** is incorrect because it would round to 500.

**100. d.** There are 30 books divided between 2 cases. Choices **a** and **b** are incorrect because the number 16 has no value in this problem. Choice **c** is incorrect because it is the wrong operation.

**101. a.** With only two sides, heads or tails, the coin would provide the least number of outcomes. Choice **b** is incorrect because a die has six potential outcomes. Choice **c** is incorrect because the spinner has three potential outcomes. Choice **d** is incorrect because the deck of cards has 52 potential outcomes.

**102. b.** The best way for students to present the information is using a line graph. Line graphs show chronological order. Choice **a** is incorrect because bar graphs are used to compare data between two or more items. Choice **c** is incorrect because $x$–$y$ plots show relationships between two or more types of data. Choice **d** is incorrect because pie charts are best to represent parts of a whole.

**103. a.** Kinesthetic learners learn best from hands-on experience. Choice **b** is incorrect because role playing is not a learning style. Choice **c** is incorrect because visual learners learn best by seeing something done. Choice **d** is incorrect because auditory learners would rather listen to things being explained than learn about them any other way.

**104. d.** Auditory learners would rather listen to things be explained than read about them. Choice **a** is incorrect because kinesthetic learners learn best from hands-on experience. Choice **b** is incorrect because tactile learners, like kinesthetic learners, learn best from experience or doing. Choice **c** is incorrect because visual learners learn best by seeing something done.

**105. b.** The teacher is demonstrating an ability to design coherent instruction that centers on the needs of the students. Choice **a** is incorrect because knowledge of a range of resources includes things like texts, instructional aids, field trips, and technology. Choice **c** is incorrect because an established environment of respect and rapport has to do with establishing relationships with students that allow the students to flourish. It could be showing appreciation, providing opportunities to get to know one another, and encouraging students to take risks. Choice **d** is incorrect because an established culture for learning has to do with setup of the classroom, display of student work, and evidence of feedback to students.

**106. a.** The best way to demonstrate knowledge of subject matter and pedagogy is to develop lessons based on best practices. Choice **b** is incorrect because goals are developed along with instructional outcomes. Choice **c** is incorrect because assessments are ways of obtaining useful feedback. Choice **d** is incorrect because demonstrating an appreciation for each individual student lends itself to creating an environment of respect and rapport, rather than knowledge of subject matter and pedagogy.

**107. a.** The teacher is demonstrating reflecting on teaching practice by thinking about parts of a lesson to see what went right and what needs improvement. Choice **b** is incorrect because professionalism has more to do with demonstrating integrity and ethical conduct through interactions with students and colleagues. Choice **c** is incorrect because professional growth and development are fostered by taking the initiative to gather research data and share best practice techniques with colleagues. Choice **d** is incorrect because it demonstrates knowledge of subject and pedagogy based on best practices, rather than assessing learning.

**108. d.** There are many reasons to make contact with parents of students in the class. The best reasons are to establish a partnership with families (choice **a**), keep parents informed about the instructional program (choice **b**), and build a sense of community (choice **c**). All of these actions support student learning.

**109. a.** The students are being asked to analyze a section of the Emancipation Proclamation. Choice **b** is incorrect because the reading standard that incorporates the use of context clues falls under craft and structure. Choice **c** is incorrect because comparing and contrasting have to do with the integration of knowledge. Choice **d** is incorrect because it refers to what students should know by the end of the year.

**110. a.** The students are being asked to recall information, which is at the lowest level. Choice **b** is incorrect because students can answer in their own words by stating facts, which is at level 2, comprehension. Choice **c** is incorrect because the question allows students to use and apply their ideas, theories, and problem-solving techniques in a new way, which requires higher-order thinking. Choice **d** is incorrect because it asks students to recall and present information, but not at the lowest level.

## Note on Scoring

Your score on this multiple-choice exam is based on the number of questions you answered correctly; there is no guessing penalty for incorrect answers and no penalty for unanswered questions. The Educational Testing Service does not set passing scores for these tests, leaving this up to the institutions, state agencies, and associations that use the tests.

First find the total number of questions you got right on the entire test. As noted earlier, questions you skipped or got wrong don't count; just add up how many questions you got right. Then, divide the number of questions you got right by the number of questions (110) to arrive at a percentage. You can check your score against the passing scores in the state or organization that requires you to take the exam.

If you are unsure of the passing score you will need, you can set yourself a goal of at least 70% of the answers right on each section of the exam. To find the percentage of questions you answered correctly, add up the number of correct answers and then divide by the total number of questions in each section to find your percentage.

What's just as important as your scores during this time of study is how you did on each of the sections tested by the exam. You need to diagnose your strengths and weaknesses so that you can concentrate your efforts as you prepare for the exam.

Use your percentage scores in conjunction with the LearningExpress Test Preparation guide in Chapter 2 of this book to help you devise a study plan. Then, turn to your study materials to work more on those sections that gave you the most trouble. You should plan to spend more time on the lessons that correspond to the questions you found hardest and less time on the lessons that correspond to areas in which you did well.

# 4 ▶ ELEMENTARY EDUCATION: CURRICULUM, INSTRUCTION, AND ASSESSMENT PRACTICE TEST 2

### CHAPTER SUMMARY

Here is the second full-length test for the Praxis II® Elementary Education: Curriculum, Instruction, and Assessment test. Now that you have taken one exam and brushed up on your studying, take this exam to see how much your score has improved.

Like Chapter 3, this chapter contains a full-length test that mirrors the Praxis II® Elementary Education: Curriculum, Instruction, and Assessment test. Though the actual test you will take might be computer-based, the question types for each exam are replicated here for you in the book.

This time, as you take this practice exam, you should simulate the actual test-taking experience as closely as you can. Find a quiet place to work where you won't be disturbed. Follow the time constraints noted at the beginning of the test.

After you finish taking your test, you should review the answer explanations. See the Note on Scoring after the last answer explanation to find information on how to score your exam.

Good luck!

1. ⓐ ⓑ ⓒ ⓓ
2. ⓐ ⓑ ⓒ ⓓ
3. ⓐ ⓑ ⓒ ⓓ
4. ⓐ ⓑ ⓒ ⓓ
5. ⓐ ⓑ ⓒ ⓓ
6. ⓐ ⓑ ⓒ ⓓ
7. ⓐ ⓑ ⓒ ⓓ
8. ⓐ ⓑ ⓒ ⓓ
9. ⓐ ⓑ ⓒ ⓓ
10. ⓐ ⓑ ⓒ ⓓ
11. ⓐ ⓑ ⓒ ⓓ
12. ⓐ ⓑ ⓒ ⓓ
13. ⓐ ⓑ ⓒ ⓓ
14. ⓐ ⓑ ⓒ ⓓ
15. ⓐ ⓑ ⓒ ⓓ
16. ⓐ ⓑ ⓒ ⓓ
17. ⓐ ⓑ ⓒ ⓓ
18. ⓐ ⓑ ⓒ ⓓ
19. ⓐ ⓑ ⓒ ⓓ
20. ⓐ ⓑ ⓒ ⓓ
21. ⓐ ⓑ ⓒ ⓓ
22. ⓐ ⓑ ⓒ ⓓ
23. ⓐ ⓑ ⓒ ⓓ
24. ⓐ ⓑ ⓒ ⓓ
25. ⓐ ⓑ ⓒ ⓓ
26. ⓐ ⓑ ⓒ ⓓ
27. ⓐ ⓑ ⓒ ⓓ
28. ⓐ ⓑ ⓒ ⓓ
29. ⓐ ⓑ ⓒ ⓓ
30. ⓐ ⓑ ⓒ ⓓ
31. ⓐ ⓑ ⓒ ⓓ
32. ⓐ ⓑ ⓒ ⓓ
33. ⓐ ⓑ ⓒ ⓓ
34. ⓐ ⓑ ⓒ ⓓ
35. ⓐ ⓑ ⓒ ⓓ
36. ⓐ ⓑ ⓒ ⓓ
37. ⓐ ⓑ ⓒ ⓓ

38. ⓐ ⓑ ⓒ ⓓ
39. ⓐ ⓑ ⓒ ⓓ
40. ⓐ ⓑ ⓒ ⓓ
41. ⓐ ⓑ ⓒ ⓓ
42. ⓐ ⓑ ⓒ ⓓ
43. ⓐ ⓑ ⓒ ⓓ
44. ⓐ ⓑ ⓒ ⓓ
45. ⓐ ⓑ ⓒ ⓓ
46. ⓐ ⓑ ⓒ ⓓ
47. ⓐ ⓑ ⓒ ⓓ
48. ⓐ ⓑ ⓒ ⓓ
49. ⓐ ⓑ ⓒ ⓓ
50. ⓐ ⓑ ⓒ ⓓ
51. ⓐ ⓑ ⓒ ⓓ
52. ⓐ ⓑ ⓒ ⓓ
53. ⓐ ⓑ ⓒ ⓓ
54. ⓐ ⓑ ⓒ ⓓ
55. ⓐ ⓑ ⓒ ⓓ
56. ⓐ ⓑ ⓒ ⓓ
57. ⓐ ⓑ ⓒ ⓓ
58. ⓐ ⓑ ⓒ ⓓ
59. ⓐ ⓑ ⓒ ⓓ
60. ⓐ ⓑ ⓒ ⓓ
61. ⓐ ⓑ ⓒ ⓓ
62. ⓐ ⓑ ⓒ ⓓ
63. ⓐ ⓑ ⓒ ⓓ
64. ⓐ ⓑ ⓒ ⓓ
65. ⓐ ⓑ ⓒ ⓓ
66. ⓐ ⓑ ⓒ ⓓ
67. ⓐ ⓑ ⓒ ⓓ
68. ⓐ ⓑ ⓒ ⓓ
69. ⓐ ⓑ ⓒ ⓓ
70. ⓐ ⓑ ⓒ ⓓ
71. ⓐ ⓑ ⓒ ⓓ
72. ⓐ ⓑ ⓒ ⓓ
73. ⓐ ⓑ ⓒ ⓓ
74. ⓐ ⓑ ⓒ ⓓ

75. ⓐ ⓑ ⓒ ⓓ
76. ⓐ ⓑ ⓒ ⓓ
77. ⓐ ⓑ ⓒ ⓓ
78. ⓐ ⓑ ⓒ ⓓ
79. ⓐ ⓑ ⓒ ⓓ
80. ⓐ ⓑ ⓒ ⓓ
81. ⓐ ⓑ ⓒ ⓓ
82. ⓐ ⓑ ⓒ ⓓ
83. ⓐ ⓑ ⓒ ⓓ
84. ⓐ ⓑ ⓒ ⓓ
85. ⓐ ⓑ ⓒ ⓓ
86. ⓐ ⓑ ⓒ ⓓ
87. ⓐ ⓑ ⓒ ⓓ
88. ⓐ ⓑ ⓒ ⓓ
89. ⓐ ⓑ ⓒ ⓓ
90. ⓐ ⓑ ⓒ ⓓ
91. ⓐ ⓑ ⓒ ⓓ
92. ⓐ ⓑ ⓒ ⓓ
93. ⓐ ⓑ ⓒ ⓓ
94. ⓐ ⓑ ⓒ ⓓ
95. ⓐ ⓑ ⓒ ⓓ
96. ⓐ ⓑ ⓒ ⓓ
97. ⓐ ⓑ ⓒ ⓓ
98. ⓐ ⓑ ⓒ ⓓ
99. ⓐ ⓑ ⓒ ⓓ
100. ⓐ ⓑ ⓒ ⓓ
101. ⓐ ⓑ ⓒ ⓓ
102. ⓐ ⓑ ⓒ ⓓ
103. ⓐ ⓑ ⓒ ⓓ
104. ⓐ ⓑ ⓒ ⓓ
105. ⓐ ⓑ ⓒ ⓓ
106. ⓐ ⓑ ⓒ ⓓ
107. ⓐ ⓑ ⓒ ⓓ
108. ⓐ ⓑ ⓒ ⓓ
109. ⓐ ⓑ ⓒ ⓓ
110. ⓐ ⓑ ⓒ ⓓ

**Time—120 minutes**
**110 Questions**

**Directions:** Each of the questions or incomplete statements that follow is followed by four suggested answers or completions. Select the one that is best in each case and fill in the corresponding lettered space on the answer sheet with a heavy, dark mark so that you cannot see the letter.

## Reading and Language Arts

1. Students in grades K–5 are supposed to be exposed to a variety of text types. Which text type falls under informational text?
   **a.** folktale
   **b.** biography
   **c.** legend
   **d.** limerick

2. The teacher asks the class to write about events in their lives that made them happy. A third-grade student writes, "The hapiest thing that ever hapened to me in my life was having a ser-prize berthday party." Which standard did the student NOT meet?
   **a.** writing
   **b.** language
   **c.** reading
   **d.** speaking

3. A first-grade teacher asks students to write a recommendation of a book for a classmate. The writing piece must have an introduction, provide text-dependent evidence, and demonstrate closure. What else must be included in the writing piece?
   **a.** Students must acknowledge alternate views.
   **b.** Students must prewrite.
   **c.** Students must state an opinion.
   **d.** Students must establish and maintain a formal style.

4. What is crucial in the process of developing reading comprehension skills?
   **a.** Have students construct mental representations of literal text.
   **b.** Enunciate mispronounced words in a timely manner.
   **c.** Reward or recognize desired reading habits.
   **d.** Communicate clear and concise expectations to students but not parents.

5. Which of the following is an effective accommodation strategy to ensure that all students have equal access to grade-level instruction?
   **a.** Do not allow extra time for written responses.
   **b.** Use recorded books or articles and text with an audio feature.
   **c.** Allow students the same amount of time to complete tests.
   **d.** Do not provide visual supports to supplement auditory lessons.

**6.** Schools have many students for whom English is not the primary language. Which of the following is effective in helping the English language learner (ELL)?
   **a.** Explain to students that bilingualism is a deficit.
   **b.** Encourage students to assimilate to this culture as quickly as possible.
   **c.** Allow students extra time for tasks and tests.
   **d.** Limit the use of academic and content-specific language.

**7.** A third-grade teacher puts "Sally sorts seashells on the seashore" on the board during a poetry lesson and asks students to notice something about what is on the board. What does the teacher want students to notice on their own?
   **a.** the hyperbole
   **b.** the consonant sound *s* being repeated
   **c.** the simile in the sentence
   **d.** the use of metaphor in the sentence

**8.** Which Common Core standard applies to answering the following question?

   *What is the antonym of* soft?

   **a.** Choose words and phrases to convey ideas precisely.
   **b.** Use context as a clue to the meaning of a word or phrase.
   **c.** Correctly use frequently confused words.
   **d.** Demonstrate understanding of words by relating them to their opposites and to words with similar but not identical meanings.

**9.** Which Common Core standard applies to answering this question?

   *Choose the sentence with the correct capitalization and punctuation.*

   **a.** Demonstrate command of the conventions of standard English grammar and usage when writing or speaking.
   **b.** Demonstrate command of the conventions of standard English capitalization, punctuation, and spelling when writing.
   **c.** Demonstrate understanding of figurative language, word relationships, and nuances in word meanings.
   **d.** Apply knowledge of language to understand how language functions in different contexts, to make effective choices for meaning or style, and to comprehend more fully when reading or listening.

**10.** A third-grade teacher just learned that the class was going to consist of two students who speak a language other than English in his classroom. All of the following strategies are effective EXCEPT which one?
   **a.** Create a predictable classroom environment where routines are established.
   **b.** Provide context for activities, like visuals and hands-on activities.
   **c.** Leave enough time for responses and provide opportunities for nonverbal responses.
   **d.** Constantly correct the students when they are answering questions.

**11.** A teacher asks her second-grade students to discuss the characters, problem, and solution for a short passage called "A Ball for My Dog." Which Common Core standard is the teacher mostly addressing?
  **a.** Follow agreed-upon rules for discussions (e.g., gaining the floor in respectful ways, listening to others with care, speaking one at a time about the topics and texts under discussion).
  **b.** Ask and answer questions about what a speaker says in order to clarify comprehension, gather additional information, or deepen understanding of a topic or issue.
  **c.** Create audio recordings of stories or poems; add drawings or other visual displays to stories or recountings of experiences when appropriate to clarify ideas, thoughts, and feelings.
  **d.** Recount or describe key ideas or details from a text read-aloud or information presented orally or through other media.

**12.** In a classroom that includes a culturally diverse group of students, learning is most likely to be enhanced if the teacher ensures that
  **a.** concepts related to cultural differences are deemphasized and conformity is stressed.
  **b.** each student is encouraged to examine issues and materials primarily from the perspective of his or her own cultural background.
  **c.** opportunities for recognizing and valuing cultural similarities and differences are integrated into all aspects of the curriculum.
  **d.** the teacher ignores or does not stress any differences of cultural diversity in the classroom.

**13.** If a teacher wanted to develop effective methods for providing information about whether students have internalized and can apply the concept developed in the lesson, which of the following assessments would be most effective?
  **a.** having each student independently prepare a definition of the concept
  **b.** asking students to create their own examples and nonexamples of the concept
  **c.** providing students with examples of the concept and asking them to use the examples correctly in original sentences
  **d.** having students select examples and nonexamples of the concept from a page of paired sentences

**14.** What is the primary reason a teacher would use a graphic organizer in class?
  **a.** It helps represent new knowledge meaningfully and visually.
  **b.** It helps keep notes and information organized.
  **c.** It allows students to go back to their notes without rereading whole texts.
  **d.** It lets students enjoy lessons and keeps them engaged.

**15.** The benefits of using graphic organizers are all of the following EXCEPT which one?
  **a.** Students are more likely to use and remember the information.
  **b.** Showing the information in an organizer can help facilitate learning.
  **c.** Students are more likely to become strategic thinkers.
  **d.** Students will learn at a faster pace than if they don't use organizers.

**16.** Many factors can impede a student's oral language production. Some simple techniques to encourage speech include all of the following EXCEPT which one?

**a.** elaborating and rephrasing when the child says something

**b.** isolating the student from activities that include oral language usage until he or she wants to join in

**c.** teaching the student the words for necessities in the school environment

**d.** offering the child audiotapes of stories that can be played and replayed

**17.** Which Common Core standard applies to answering this question?

*The canal was so **parched** that the fish lined up with their towels to take turns swimming in the few remaining water holes.*

*What is the meaning of the word* parched *in this sentence?*

**a.** Use context as a clue to the meaning of a word or phrase.

**b.** Interpret figures of speech.

**c.** Use knowledge of language and its conventions when writing, speaking, reading, or listening.

**d.** Distinguish among the connotations (associations) of words with similar denotations (definitions).

**18.** When an English language learner participates in an oral discussion in class and mispronounces a word, the teacher should

**a.** be sure to correct each mispronunciation orally and at the time of the mistake so that the learner will not repeat it.

**b.** ask the student to write the mispronounced word down so that he or she can see it visually.

**c.** model using the mispronounced word correctly in the discussion but do not correct the pronunciation immediately after the speaker says the word.

**d.** point out the error and immediately do a mini-lesson on it for the whole class.

**19.** A new teacher wants to make sure that she has a well-managed classroom for the upcoming school year. She has organized her classroom and supplies and planned for instructional activities for the first week of school, and has a plan for dealing with problem behaviors. What is the main reason the teacher has made sure these strategies are in place?

**a.** The teacher realizes that the classroom environment and student behavior expectations are necessary for an effective learning environment.

**b.** The teacher thinks it is necessary to have an organized plan for the school year.

**c.** The teacher wants to make sure the students are not distracted during the school day.

**d.** The teacher wants to convey to her class that she is in charge of the class.

**20.** Teachers tend to present new knowledge linguistically. The teacher usually talks and the students take notes, and there is little opportunity to create visuals. What can the teacher do to teach a concept that is complex by trying to use visuals?
- **a.** Use graphic organizers
- **b.** Use the word wall
- **c.** Use context clues
- **d.** Use informal reading inventories

**21.** A kindergarten teacher gives the students a worksheet with an image and boxes below it.

What strategy is the teacher using?
- **a.** word building
- **b.** word families
- **c.** Elkonin boxes
- **d.** sight words

**22.** Elkonin boxes can help students understand phonemic awareness in all of the following ways EXCEPT which one?
- **a.** They can help students with decoding and spelling skills.
- **b.** They can help the students count the phonemes in a word.
- **c.** They can help the students with reading comprehension.
- **d.** They can help segment words into syllables.

**23.** Here is an example of a teacher presenting the poem "Dream Variation" by Langston Hughes.

*To fling my arms wide*
*In some place of the sun,*
*To whirl and to dance*
*Till the white day is done.*

Teacher: *I'm picturing a young girl with bare feet in a summer dress twirling in her front yard with her arms stretched outward.*

*Then rest at cool evening*
*Beneath a tall tree*

Teacher: *I'm picturing a large willow tree and the young girl sitting underneath it.*

*While night comes on gently,*
*Dark like me—*

Teacher: *I'm now going back to my original picture of the young girl and can add more detail to the image of the girl and what she may look like.*

What technique is the teacher using?
- **a.** story structure
- **b.** read-aloud
- **c.** think-aloud
- **d.** modeling

**24.** What is the primary reason for a word wall?
- **a.** to have students find words that are difficult for them
- **b.** to increase sight words for students and have them use those words in their environment
- **c.** to have students copy words in their vocabulary notebooks
- **d.** to allow students to make connections between topics learned in class and the new word

**25.** A teacher wants to incorporate a word wall into his instruction. All of the following can help him use word walls to help enhance instruction EXCEPT which one?

**a.** Teachers and students should work together to determine which words should go on the word wall; try to include words that children use most commonly in their writing.

**b.** Use the word wall daily to practice words, incorporating a variety of activities such as chanting, snapping, cheering, clapping, tracing, and word guessing games, as well as writing them.

**c.** Words should be selected at random.

**d.** Word walls should be referred to often so students come to understand and see their relevance.

**26.** Some implications from Stephen Krashen's theory for classroom learning for English language learners are all of the following EXCEPT which one?

**a.** Grammar should not be taught in isolation.

**b.** The learner must feel secure and unthreatened in the learning environment.

**c.** The teachers should use scaffolding techniques such as visuals, realia, and graphic organizers.

**d.** Quickly correct students when they make mistakes using the language.

**27.** A first-grade teacher wants to conduct a choral reading with the class. How does this help with reluctant and struggling readers?

**a.** It can provide less skilled readers the opportunity to practice and receive support before being required to read on their own.

**b.** It can provide students an opportunity to participate in class activities.

**c.** It can help students follow reading patterns.

**d.** It can help students understand where mistakes are being made when reading.

**28.** Using this image, what is the teacher teaching the class?

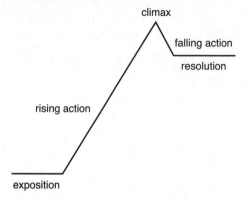

**a.** text structure

**b.** story structure

**c.** literature circles

**d.** literary genres

**29.** A teacher is reading a novel with the class and a word comes up that the class does not understand. Which of the following should the teacher do to use this moment to review context clues?

**a.** Have a student look up the definition.

**b.** Ask a student to spell the word and look up the definition afterward.

**c.** Give the students another example using the word.

**d.** Give students the origin of the word.

**30.** A first-grade class is asked to figure out the meaning of the word *lanky*. Which is an example of a sentence that provides context clues?

**a.** The lanky girl stood by the chalkboard smiling from ear to ear.

**b.** Don't touch the lanky bug with the stick.

**c.** She waved good-bye to the lanky boy standing all alone at the bus stop.

**d.** The lanky basketball player was able to squeeze through the narrow opening as he ducked to get through the doorway.

**31.** Skimming is a useful technique to teach students. All are benefits of skimming EXCEPT which of the following?
 **a.** It can give a more accurate picture of text to be read later.
 **b.** Skimming is useful for reviewing text already read.
 **c.** Skimming is most often used for quickly reading material.
 **d.** It can save time rather than reading the whole text.

**32.** A student is looking in an article to find information about Thomas Alva Edison's patent date for the lightbulb. What technique should he use?
 **a.** skimming
 **b.** prereading
 **c.** summarizing
 **d.** scanning

**33.** A teacher conducts literacy conferences with students in her class. She has a group of English language learners who do not speak English. It is recommended that she
 **a.** ask the students to wait to confer with her until another student who speaks the same language is available to join them.
 **b.** put all of the English language learners together and have a group conference.
 **c.** spend some time teaching the words using pictures or objects in the room until the students feel comfortable.
 **d.** spend only one or two minutes with each of the students since they can't understand.

**34.** A teacher is faced with a situation in which parents come to him and accuse him of treating their child unfairly in class. Which of the following should the teacher NOT do?
 **a.** The teacher should set up a meeting with the student and the parents.
 **b.** The teacher should review his interactions with the student during the year.
 **c.** The teacher should ask the school administrator to deal with the situation.
 **d.** The teacher should sit with the parents and the student and determine some solutions to find common ground.

**35.** Which Common Core standard applies to answering this question?

 *An **opportunistic** animal is one that*
 _____.

 **a.** Cite textual evidence to support analysis of what the text says explicitly as well as inferences drawn from the text.
 **b.** Determine an author's point of view or purpose in a text and explain how it is conveyed in the text.
 **c.** Use knowledge of language and its conventions when writing, speaking, reading, or listening.
 **d.** Determine the meaning of words and phrases as they are used in a text, including figurative, connotative, and technical meanings.

**36.** A teacher wants to use multiple intelligences framework to provide a variety of choice reading projects for students. Which is an example of a project that might be geared toward the naturalist intelligence?
**a.** Create a comic book to represent the story.
**b.** Create a graphic organizer that shows the plot development of the story.
**c.** Write a rap or a song for the major character to sing.
**d.** Identify the main character with a signature flower, plant, tree, or animal and explain.

**37.** To understand specific text structures, a teacher gives her students this graphic organizer.

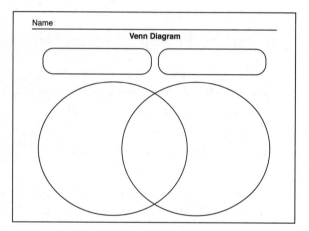

What is the teacher teaching the students?
**a.** cause and effect
**b.** problem and solution
**c.** sequence
**d.** compare and contrast

**38.** Which of the following best describes a narrative?
**a.** It records a person's thoughts, feelings, and observations.
**b.** It consists of character, setting, conflict, and plot.
**c.** It usually begins with a statement of the position taken by the author with arguments and evidence to back up the position.
**d.** It creates an impression of a person, place, event, feeling, or idea.

# Mathematics

**39.** A fourth-grade teacher puts the following problem on the board: *Write in standard form: 6 thousands + 5 tens + 8 ones*. Hansel answers 6,085. What did he do wrong?
**a.** He forgot the hundreds.
**b.** He subtracted.
**c.** He wrote it in word form.
**d.** He switched the values for the tens and ones place.

**40.** A fourth-grade teacher is going to teach about angles in class. What can she use to introduce this topic?
**a.** money
**b.** clocks
**c.** multiplication facts
**d.** patterns

**41.** A sixth-grade teacher gives the class the following problem: $(12 \times 3 + 12) \div 6 + 2$. What step should be taught first?
**a.** $3 + 12$
**b.** $6 + 2$
**c.** $12 \times 3$
**d.** $12 \times 12$

**42.** A teacher asks her fifth-grade class to round 3,201,002 to the nearest hundred thousand. He calls on Elaine, who answers, "3,000,000." What did she do wrong?
   **a.** She did not grasp the concept of rounding.
   **b.** She confused the millions and hundred thousands places.
   **c.** She confused the hundred thousands and ten thousands places.
   **d.** She rounded up instead of down.

**43.** A teacher asks her second-grade class, "How many inches are there in two feet?" What prior knowledge must the students have in order to solve this?
   **a.** how many feet in an inch
   **b.** how big an inch is
   **c.** how many inches in one foot
   **d.** how many feet in a yard

**44.** The teacher asks students to skip count to find the number that comes next: 45, 54, 63, __. When would teaching students to skip count be an effective mathematical technique?
   **a.** Skip counting is best taught in conjunction with division.
   **b.** Skip counting is best taught in conjunction with multiplication.
   **c.** Skip counting is best taught in conjunction with addition.
   **d.** Skip counting is best taught in conjunction with subtraction.

**45.** By how much would the value 53 change if the digit 5 were replaced by the digit 8?
   **a.** 3
   **b.** 8
   **c.** 30
   **d.** 80

**46.** A kindergarten teacher is instructing the students about symmetry as they learn to write uppercase letters. Which letter shape has one vertical line of symmetry?
   **a.** B
   **b.** C
   **c.** A
   **d.** K

**47.** Mrs. Howell has been told that she calls on more girls than boys. The principal would like to see her call on more boys. Mrs. Howell argues there are 23 students in class and 14 of them are girls. Therefore, it is more likely she will call on a girl. What is Mrs. Howell most likely basing her argument on?
   **a.** common sense since there are more girls in the class
   **b.** research that girls know more than boys
   **c.** probability based on the number of girls to boys
   **d.** rational thinking, which states her actions were flawless

**48.** A second-grade teacher asks his class to estimate how long the school building is. What must he teach them prior to this task?
   **a.** units of measuring mass and examples
   **b.** units of measuring distance and examples
   **c.** units of measuring capacity and examples
   **d.** how many classrooms are in the school

**49.** A teacher put this problem on the board for a second-grade class: *I left my house at 8:40. I drove for 25 minutes to get to school. What time did I get to school?* Alex answered, "8:65." What did Alex do wrong?
   **a.** He added.
   **b.** He subtracted.
   **c.** He guessed.
   **d.** He did not know that there are only 60 minutes in an hour.

**50.** Joe wants to build a doghouse; however, the lumber he needs to build the doghouse is sold only in 6-foot lengths. Joe needs 43 feet of lumber to build the doghouse. How many feet of lumber will he need to buy?
   **a.** 42
   **b.** 43
   **c.** 40
   **d.** 48

**51.** A first-grade teacher asks her class to find the sum of 3 + 4 and then check it using the inverse operation. How would this be shown?
   **a.** 7 − 4 = 3
   **b.** 4 + 3 = 7
   **c.** 3 + 4 = 7
   **d.** 3 − 4 = 7

**52.** A fifth-grade teacher gives this problem: 24 + 5.5; Joe answers, "7.9." What did he do wrong?
   **a.** He subtracted.
   **b.** He didn't line up the decimal places when he added.
   **c.** He added.
   **d.** He divided.

**53.** A fifth-grade teacher puts the following problem on the board: *What are the lengths of the sides of a square with a perimeter of 28 feet?* Which student answer is correct?
   **a.** 112 feet
   **b.** 32 feet
   **c.** 24 feet
   **d.** 7 feet

**54.** Thomas has a total of 54 apples. There are 6 apples in each bag. Which step can be used to find how many bags of apples Thomas has?
   **a.** 54 + 6
   **b.** 54 − 6
   **c.** 54 × 6
   **d.** 54 ÷ 6

**55.** Kendall is going hiking. She has packed enough supplies to last for 2 days. She packed 9 water bottles, 15 health food bars, and 10 cans of food. Which equation shows how Kendall found the number of items she could eat and drink each day?
   **a.** 2 × 16
   **b.** 19 ÷ 2
   **c.** 2 × 34
   **d.** 34 ÷ 2

**56.** Fourth-grade students drill multiplication tables for 5 minutes a day after lunch. Why does the teacher drill multiplication tables?
   **a.** The teacher is practicing mastery of basic math facts.
   **b.** The teacher is instilling a routine for students.
   **c.** The teacher is helping the students to settle in for the afternoon.
   **d.** The teacher is preparing students for division.

**57.** What must be taught prior to $\frac{1}{2} + \frac{3}{4}$?
   **a.** Find the least common multiple.
   **b.** Add the fractions.
   **c.** Multiply the least common denominator by the numerator and denominator.
   **d.** Find numerators and denominators.

**58.** Which would be a part of an introductory lesson teaching second graders long division?
   **a.** The first digit of the divisor is divided by the dividend.
   **b.** Place the whole number result above the dividing line on top of the first number; ignore any remainders.
   **c.** Bring down the next digit of the dividend.
   **d.** Check answer by multiplying divisor by result to see if it equals dividend.

**59.** What must the fourth-grade class master to simplify the fraction $\frac{6}{8}$?
   **a.** the greatest common factor of two numbers
   **b.** multiples of 2
   **c.** dividing the numerator and denominator by the greatest common multiple
   **d.** vocabulary associated with fractions

**60.** Why should the teacher instruct students to use placeholders when doing long division?
   **a.** The number value will be different without a placeholder.
   **b.** The students will lose their placeout with a placeholder.
   **c.** The students will be unable to check their answers.
   **d.** The place value makes for neater, more organized presentation of student ideas.

# Science

**61.** A second-grade class has a class pet. Students are expected take the class pet home during the weekends and holidays. What could be the instructional objective for this?
   **a.** Students will learn respect and responsibility for living beings.
   **b.** Students will learn the importance of collaboration and trust.
   **c.** Students will understand how all living things are connected.
   **d.** Students will understand why all living things are dependent upon one another.

**62.** Students in a third-grade class are asked to choose a mammal and create a diorama. What should be included in the diorama?
   **a.** the animal living in outer space
   **b.** the animal's evolutionary tree
   **c.** the mammal's entire ecosystem
   **d.** other mammals that live in the same terrain

**63.** Prior to having students do a science experiment, the scientific method is taught. How will the scientific method help students in developing a science experiment?
   **a.** It will help them prove the hypothesis is correct.
   **b.** It will help them do an experiment that can be repeated.
   **c.** It is a proven method for disproving inaccuracies.
   **d.** It will provide guidelines for predicting the outcome of an experiment.

**64.** The teacher gives students a sealed box with an item in it. The students are to make an educated guess about what is in the box. They can shake it but cannot open it. What is mostly being taught?
   **a.** a guess
   **b.** experimental methods
   **c.** conceptual thinking
   **d.** problem solving

**65.** The teacher has students use various kinds of soda to clean a penny. Which unit would this demonstration fall under?
   **a.** life science
   **b.** earth science
   **c.** physical science
   **d.** health

**66.** The teacher provides the students with a chart of the scientific names of butterflies. Students are to sort the chart into domain, kingdom, phylum, class, order, family, genus, and species. What scientific process is being taught?
   **a.** language and communication
   **b.** order/hierarchy
   **c.** growth
   **d.** testing hypotheses

**67.** Which would be the best way for the teacher to visually demonstrate classification?
 **a.** pie graph
 **b.** inverted triangle
 **c.** bar graph
 **d.** line graph

**68.** Organisms are made of one or more cells. Cells are the units of structure and function of a living thing. Cells are composed of organelles. Why are cells important to emphasize in instruction?
 **a.** Cells are not important when teaching life science.
 **b.** Cells are the building blocks of life.
 **c.** Only some organisms have cells.
 **d.** All cells have the same physical characteristics.

**69.**

A     B     C

Students are given these pictures and asked to identify which is the gas. A student chooses picture A as the gas. What can the teacher assume the student does NOT know?

 **a.** that a gas has a definite volume and definite shape
 **b.** that a gas has a definite volume, not shape
 **c.** that a gas has a definite shape, not volume
 **d.** that a gas does not have a definite shape or volume

**70.** The teacher tells the students that solids vibrate, or move slowly, giving them a compact or solid state. Think of the properties of a rock in terms of volume and shape. What does this say about solids?
 **a.** Solids are heavy.
 **b.** Solids have a definite shape and volume.
 **c.** Solids can take the shape of the container they are placed in.
 **d.** Some fluids are considered solids.

**71.** A teacher tells the students that energy cannot be destroyed. In a demonstrated clip, the students are shown a moving car hitting a parked car. The reaction causes the parked car to move. The parked car moves because energy has been transferred. What law of energy is being taught by the demonstration?
 **a.** law of conservation of energy
 **b.** law of thermodynamics
 **c.** momentum
 **d.** mechanics

## Social Studies

**72.** During a geography lesson, the teacher asks students to find the shortest route between New York and Japan. Students are given a choice to use a map or globe to find their answer. Why would the teacher give students a choice rather than choose for them?
 **a.** The teacher is allowing students to choose as a means of enhancing student motivation and interest in task.
 **b.** The teacher is demonstrating flexibility.
 **c.** The teacher is building cognitive effort in students by having students weigh alternatives.
 **d.** The teacher is allowing students to incorporate their own experiences into the learning process.

**73.** A fifth-grade teacher wants to deepen students' understanding of cultural blending. Which would enhance students' experience of cultural blending?
  **a.** researching the spread of democracy to many areas of the globe
  **b.** reading the narrative about the *Mayflower* landing in Plymouth, Massachusetts
  **c.** analyzing how the English language has many root words from other languages
  **d.** explaining how immigrants are a vital part of the American economy

**74.** A fifth-grade class is studying slavery in America. Which of the following assumptions is NOT valid for the teacher to make prior to the lesson?
  **a.** The students will see how slavery has shaped the lives of the slave and enslaver.
  **b.** The African American students will share the same perspective regarding slavery.
  **c.** The students will understand the view of the abolitionists.
  **d.** The students will learn what it means to own another person.

**75.** A fifth-grade teacher is having students dress up and recite from memory the works of famous American female poets during Women's History Month. What is most likely the teacher's instructional objective?
  **a.** to stress the importance of emphasizing different words
  **b.** to abridge students' experience and exposure to time under study
  **c.** to increase students' higher-order thinking skills through presentation techniques
  **d.** to understand expressive, communicative, and reading skills through memorization

**76.** Which essential question would have the students respond using historical/social studies strategies?
  **a.** What was the authors' purpose in writing the Constitution?
  **b.** Was everyone in the American colonies treated fairly?
  **c.** Was the setting in Lois Lowry's novel *Number the Stars* realistic?
  **d.** What is the likelihood that someone's ethnicity will be identified through observation?

**77.** A first-grade teacher wants students to understand how their community relates to their state. Which would be the best demonstration for the teacher to use?
  **a.** Chart the responsibilities of county, local, and state governments.
  **b.** Identify authority figures in the home, school, and community.
  **c.** Recite the Pledge of Allegiance.
  **d.** Explain the reasons for recognizing national holidays.

**78.** The teacher wants students to know that social studies are the study of societies intended to promote civic competence. Which is an example of a civic competence lesson?
  **a.** the major arguments expressed in the Federalist Papers.
  **b.** the teaching of the constitutional principles
  **c.** the teaching of the roles of the immigrants prior to the Civil War
  **d.** the factors that contributed to national unity

**79.** A second-grade class is studying the relationship between the Native Americans and colonists. The teacher holds up a picture of the first Thanksgiving and asks students if they recognize anything about the picture. One child responds by saying there are Indians and Pilgrims in the picture. What should happen next?

**a.** The teacher should ask if other students agree with the one student who responded.

**b.** The teacher should correct the student and say "Indians" are "Native Americans."

**c.** The teacher should ask for more details in the picture.

**d.** The teacher should ask where the Pilgrims came from.

**80.** The teacher provides second-grade students with cutouts of the seven continents. The cutouts make it possible for students to puzzle together the continent pieces, making one large body of land. What impact should this lesson have on students' learning?

**a.** Lesson should stimulate judgments.

**b.** Lesson should activate analysis of relationships.

**c.** Lesson should produce alternatives.

**d.** Lesson should activate perception.

**81.** The teacher asks students to compare and contrast the New Deal with the Progressive reform movements. Which theme does this align with?

**a.** economic systems

**b.** human movement

**c.** civic values

**d.** government systems

**82.** Prior to studying about early people's movements, the teacher asks students to predict how early people traveled from Asia to North America. What is the purpose of asking students to make a prediction?

**a.** to activate knowledge

**b.** to activate comprehension

**c.** to activate analysis

**d.** to activate synthesis

## Arts and Physical Education

**83.** A first-grade music teacher wants students to understand quarter notes prior to playing on an instrument. Which children's game will help students understand quarter notes?

**a.** tic-tac-toe

**b.** hide and seek

**c.** tag

**d.** red light, green light

**84.** The music teacher has first-grade students clap the pulse of a word while saying it. For example, the students would clap the pulse *pine-ap-ple* for *pineapple*. What is the reason for the teacher doing this?

**a.** to get students to understand when a long note is needed

**b.** to get students to understand how measures are extended

**c.** to get students to understand how a symphony is made

**d.** to get students to understand rhythm

**85.** A music teacher wants to show third-grade students how they can learn the keys of the piano easily. The students are told the piano keys are named for the first seven letters of the alphabet. The teacher asks students to label the piano keys. What is the teacher checking for?
a. application
b. comprehension
c. knowledge
d. analysis

**86.** The art teacher shows students drawings of fruit on a table. What is the teacher instructing on?
a. still life
b. abstract
c. portrait
d. collage

**87.** When colors like red and green are opposite each other on a color wheel, the colors are said to be _____.
a. primary
b. complementary
c. secondary
d. analogous

**88.** The teacher is working to build endurance in students before a physical activity assessment. What will be the outcome for students?
a. They will be able to jump higher.
b. They will be able to lift heavier objects.
c. They will be able to run longer.
d. They will be able to recover more quickly.

**89.** How much sleep does the body need to revitalize itself?
a. seven hours
b. ten hours
c. four hours
d. eight hours

**90.** Why is it important to exercise?
a. to build strong muscles
b. to improve overall health
c. to keep weight down
d. all of the above

**91.** Which refers to how often a person exercises?
a. frequency
b. intensity
c. time
d. type

**92.** Which refers to cardiovascular or resistance training?
a. frequency
b. intensity
c. time
d. type

**93.** Which refers to a good balance to ensure that the workout is difficult enough to challenge the body without overtraining, injury, or burnout?
a. frequency
b. intensity
c. time
d. type

# General

**94.** A second-grade teacher gives the students a summative assessment at the end of the unit. Most students fall below the teacher's expectations. What should the teacher do?
  **a.** The teacher should inform parents that students are not reaching expectations to gain support and have students improve.
  **b.** The teacher should collect various forms of data to investigate questions about students' work, teacher practices, and learning.
  **c.** The teacher should give a formative assessment.
  **d.** The teacher should tell students they will be given the summative assessment again in two days, and then wait and see if they do better.

**95.** Which is a demonstration of an interdisciplinary lesson?
  **a.** During a social studies lesson, the teacher tells students that radiocarbon dating is used to identify the age of a living thing. Everything that is and was living has radiocarbon in it. Students are to demonstrate an understanding of radiocarbon dating.
  **b.** During a study of early writers, students are taught to use quills.
  **c.** During a study of rock formations, radiocarbon dating was used to identify the age of each layer.
  **d.** The teacher designs groups so that the above-average students are placed in groups with average and below-average students. The students are asked to work together to solve the mystery of cave drawings.

**96.** A teacher is trying to create a lesson that is relevant to the students. Which of the following is NOT true about making a lesson relevant?
  **a.** Students learn how to use information in a relevant manner through modeling and discussion.
  **b.** Relevant, meaningful activities engage students and connect to what they already know, allowing for ease of memorizing.
  **c.** Relevant lessons answer the question "Why do I have to learn this?"
  **d.** Students are able to make connections to the material being taught.

**97.** Which is the most effective form of teaching for heightened student engagement?
  **a.** teacher-centered
  **b.** parallel teaching
  **c.** station teaching
  **d.** student-centered

**98.** It is important for teachers to be familiar with teaching and learning. Research states that students are able to retain more information learned
  **a.** by what they do.
  **b.** by what is heard.
  **c.** by what is read.
  **d.** by what is observed.

**99.** What do these types of instructional methods—learning centers, tiered lessons, multiple intelligences—have in common?
  **a.** Teachers are provided with a more detailed perspective of student learning.
  **b.** Students are given an opportunity to work independently.
  **c.** The responsibility for learning is placed on the student.
  **d.** The methods work best for instructing diverse groups of learners.

**100.** A third-grade teacher has created a tiered lesson on the ways to prepare for natural disasters. Which is NOT a reason for the teacher to tier a lesson?
   **a.** Tiered lessons allow the teacher to present a concept at varied levels of complexity.
   **b.** Tiered lessons allow the teacher to engage students' varied learning styles.
   **c.** Tiered lessons allow the teacher to assign different tasks within the same lesson based on student readiness and learning style.
   **d.** Tiered lessons allow teachers more time for instruction because there is no need for an assessment when the lesson is created with student readiness, learning style, and interest level.

**101.** Which would be the most favorable way of teaching about the Revolutionary War?
   **a.** Have students use the textbook to read and take notes of events that led to the Revolutionary War.
   **b.** Have students read and analyze the Declaration of Independence.
   **c.** Have students watch a video on the Revolutionary War.
   **d.** Have students research the topic on the Internet.

**102.** Describe what is meant by the quote: "Students should understand that 'fair' means that everyone gets what they need and not everyone will get the same thing."
   **a.** It is a teacher's response to students saying, "It's not fair!"
   **b.** It means teachers should treat students fairly by not treating them the same.
   **c.** It means teachers should treat everyone the same.
   **d.** It means that a teacher is confused about the meaning of equal and fair.

**103.** A third-grade teacher wants to teach about parallel lines. Which real-world example would be best?
   **a.** intersection
   **b.** sidewalk
   **c.** road
   **d.** railroad tracks

**104.** The teacher wants to arrange the class into cooperative groups. What is the ideal size for a group?
   **a.** six
   **b.** four
   **c.** three
   **d.** five

**105.** Authentic assessment can serve all of the following purposes EXCEPT
   **a.** emphasizing what students know, rather than don't know.
   **b.** testing collective abilities of the student.
   **c.** testing an isolated skill of the student.
   **d.** eliciting higher-order thinking.

**106.** A Venn diagram is poorly suited to which of the following?
   **a.** displaying sequential order
   **b.** showing common themes
   **c.** comparing information
   **d.** contrasting information

**107.** Which one of the following educational theories would be consistent with an environment that promotes discovery?
   **a.** behaviorist
   **b.** social constructivist
   **c.** cognitive constructivist
   **d.** activist

**108.** During which of the following steps in direct instruction is a teacher most likely to activate students' background knowledge and focus attention?
  **a.** presenting of new material
  **b.** reviewing previously learned material
  **c.** guided practice
  **d.** independent practice

**109.** Students in a first-grade class are given a spelling pretest prior to starting the vocabulary words for the week. What is the purpose of giving a pretest?
  **a.** to create a word association
  **b.** for recall of rules for spelling
  **c.** to learn how to sound out words
  **d.** to identify words that are known and unknown

**110.** Classroom rules are being discussed and developed. Students are asked to contribute to the rules. Why have students been asked to contribute to class rules?
  **a.** to ensure student buy-in
  **b.** to establish a collaborative environment
  **c.** to ensure all rules are known
  **d.** to establish a community of learning

# Answers and Explanations

## Reading and Language Arts

**1. b.** Biography is a form of informational text. Choices **a**, **c**, and **d** are forms of literature.

**2. b.** The student did not demonstrate command of the conventions of standard English capitalization, punctuation, and spelling when writing. The student did follow the instruction of the teacher and write about an experience meeting writing standards as in choice **a**. Students were not asked to read anything or to present, so choices **c** and **d** are irrelevant.

**3. c.** The students should state an opinion of the book. Choice **a** is incorrect because alternate views are used to balance a piece. Choice **b** is incorrect because a prewrite does not need to be included in the writing piece. Choice **d** is incorrect because there is not just one way to write as long as the conventions of English are followed.

**4. a.** It is important to teach students to construct mental representations as they read to gain better understanding via mental visualization. Choice **b** is incorrect because it is more important to understand than to enunciate words when reading. Choice **c** is incorrect because it is not specific enough in describing what desired reading habits would be rewarded or recognized. Choice **d** is incorrect because teachers need open communication with students as well as parents.

**5. b.** We need to provide students appropriate accommodations to demonstrate or communicate what they have learned. Choice **a** is incorrect because it is important to provide extra time for students who deserve time to complete tasks. Choice **c** is incorrect because some students may require extra time according to their individual education plans (IEPs) or if they are English language learners. Choice **d** is incorrect because it is important to provide visual supports to all learners.

**6. c.** English language learners need extra time to process what is said to them, translate into their native language, and then translate back into English. Choice **a** is incorrect because we need to embrace the fact that bilingualism is an asset and not a deficit. Choice **b** is incorrect because we need to allow students to share their customs and use the language reflective of their culture. Choice **d** is incorrect because teachers need to immerse students in a literacy-rich environment in order for them to learn the English language.

**7. b.** The consonant sound *s* is being repeated in the line. Choice **a** is incorrect because there is no exaggeration in the line. Choice **c** is incorrect because the line is not comparing two things using *like* or *as*. Choice **d** is incorrect because the line is not comparing two unlike things.

**8. d.** Students need to understand the opposite of the meaning of the word *soft*. Choice **a** is incorrect because students are not being asked to pick a word to convey ideas. Choice **b** is incorrect because students are not looking for context clues to determine the meaning of an unknown word. Choice **c** is incorrect because *soft* is not a word that is frequently confused.

**9. b.** The question asks the students to understand the conventions of English, including capitalization and punctuation. Choice **a** is incorrect because the question does not ask students to understand the conventions of English grammar. Choice **c** is incorrect because the question is not asking to have students understand figurative language, meanings, or relationships. Choice **d** is incorrect because the question is not asking students to apply knowledge of the language when reading or listening.

**10. d.** Constant correction of the students' speech will stifle their communication. The teacher should check his or her comprehension of what the student says and repeat and rephrase questions and answers. Choices **a**, **b**, and **c** are all good strategies to help a student feel more comfortable in an English-only classroom.

**11. d.** The teacher is asking students to recall details from the story and to present them orally. Choice **a** is incorrect because students are doing more than just discussing the question; the teacher is looking for students to answer specific aspects of the question. Choice **b** is incorrect because students are not asking questions about a speaker. Choice **c** is incorrect because the students are not asked to create audio recordings of stories or poems.

**12. c.** This allows students to feel comfortable in the class and still value their backgrounds. Choice **a** does not allow students to bring in their own background information and knowledge into the classroom, and sends the message that everyone needs to be the same, which we are not. Choice **b** does not allow students to see and examine the perspectives of other cultural backgrounds. Choice **d** is not realistic, and the teacher needs to be able to handle and learn about the diversity in his or her classroom.

**13. b.** This shows that the teacher understands how to use varied assessment strategies to enhance student learning. Choices **a** and **c** show that the teacher lacks the ability to modify assessments based on the student's ability. Choice **d** does not allow students to enhance their learning.

**14. a.** A graphic organizer helps the students use the information and helps facilitate their understanding of the topic. Choice **b** is incorrect because although a graphic organizer does organize the information, that is not the primary reason for using it. Choice **c** is incorrect because although students can use the organizer to look back at notes taken, that is not its primary purpose. Choice **d** is incorrect; although students do enjoy using graphic organizers, it is not the primary reason for using them.

**15. d.** We cannot say that students will learn material faster, but the information will become more comprehensible. Choices **a**, **b**, and **c** are all benefits of using graphic organizers.

**16. b.** It is not helpful to the student if he or she is kept away from class activities that can help in oral language production. Choices **a**, **c**, and **d** are all good techniques to use for the student.

**17. a.** Students need to look at the surrounding text to figure out that there was almost no water left in the canal. Choice **b** is incorrect because students do not have to figure out the figure of speech in the question. Choice **c** is incorrect because students are not asked to understand language conventions. Choice **d** is incorrect because the question does not ask students to understand words that have similar meanings.

**18. c.** The teacher does not want to make the child feel uncomfortable when he or she is participating in class discussion, but the teacher needs to note the mistake, correct it, and model it for the student. Choices **a**, **b**, and **d** are incorrect because they can make the student feel uncomfortable and insecure about the mispronunciation, and he or she may not participate in class discussions again.

**19. a.** The teacher knows that an effective classroom is important to support learning and create worthwhile activities to allow students to be highly involved. Choices **b**, **c**, and **d** are important, but the main reason to have effective classroom management is to keep expectations in place that create a sound learning environment.

**20. a.** Graphic organizers can help students understand complex topics in a visual representation. Choice **b** is incorrect because it does not help a student understand a topic, but it can help in vocabulary use. Choice **c** is incorrect because context clues do not help students understand a complex topic. Choice **d** is incorrect because reading inventories do not help visualize a topic.

**21. c.** The image shows Elkonin boxes that are used to teach phonemic awareness. Choices **a**, **b**, and **d** are incorrect because the image does not represent word building, word families, or sight words, respectively.

**22. c.** Elkonin boxes do not help with reading comprehension. Choices **a**, **b**, and **d** are all reasons why Elkonin boxes help in phonemic awareness.

**23. c.** After every stanza the teacher is explaining to students what she is thinking and how she makes inferences. Choice **a** is incorrect because she is not teaching story structure. Choice **b** is incorrect because the teacher is not just reading the poem aloud. Choice **d** is incorrect because the teacher is not just modeling; the teacher is reflecting on the thinking that goes along with understanding text.

**24. b.** Word walls help increase the use of previously unknown vocabulary words, and they also support students who are struggling with vocabulary. Choice **a** is incorrect because students are going to put up words that are difficult, but it has to be done as a class. Choice **c** is incorrect because students are not just copying the words; they must be able to use the words. Choice **d** is incorrect because students are not just making connections to topics; they need to use the words frequently in other discussions.

**25. c.** Words should be chosen based on the content-area material in the curriculum so that students can use the words frequently. Choices **a**, **b**, and **d** are all ways to help enhance instruction.

**26. d.** Learners may not be able to understand the corrections until they are developmentally ready. Teachers should not overemphasize corrections during instruction. Choices **a**, **b**, and **c** are all examples of implications of Krashen's theory of language acquisition.

**27. a.** Choral reading does help practice reading and also provides a fluency model when the teacher is reading. Choice **b** is incorrect because students have other opportunities to participate in classroom activities. Choice **c** is incorrect because although it may help with reading patterns, that is not the primary purpose. Choice **d** is incorrect because the purpose of choral reading is not to point out mistakes being made by the student.

**28. b.** The image is an example of a story structure. Choices **a**, **c**, and **d** are incorrect because the image does not depict text structure, literature circles, or literary genres.

**29. c.** The teacher is using this opportunity to have students figure out the word's meaning in context. Choices **a**, **b**, and **d** are incorrect because they don't allow the students to use the words in context.

**30. d.** The sentence gives context that *lanky* means tall and thin. Choices **a**, **b**, and **c** do not give the impression of the meaning of *lanky*.

**31. d.** The benefit of skimming is not to avoid reading the whole text; it is a prereading technique that can be used with students. Choices **a**, **b**, and **c** are all examples of the benefits of teaching skimming.

**32. d.** Scanning is used to locate a specific fact or detail in a text. Choice **a** is incorrect because skimming is used to get a general overview of the text. Choice **b** is incorrect because the student is not using prereading techniques to find the information in the text. Choice **c** is incorrect because the student does not need to summarize the selection.

**33. b.** This choice does not make the students feel like they are left out in any of the classroom activities and allows them to try to talk to the teacher. Choices **a**, **c**, and **d** are incorrect because they can make students feel like they do not belong to the class.

**34. c.** The teacher needs to speak and deal with the parents first and try to resolve the issue with them. If the parents, teacher, and student cannot resolve the issue, then the teacher should invite an administrator to serve as a facilitator in another meeting. Choices **a**, **b**, and **d** are good ways to handle the situation with the parents and student.

**35. d.** Because the reader should use the clues in the context to find the definition, this choice would be the most appropriate standard. Choice **a** asks the reader to find explicit information in the text, so this standard would not fit the question. Choice **b** is incorrect because the question does not ask about the author's point of view, and choice **c** does not fit because the reader does not need to know the language's conventions when reading to determine the vocabulary word.

**36. d.** The naturalist intelligence uses items in nature to express understanding. Choice **a** is incorrect because it applies to the visual intelligence. Choice **b** is incorrect because it applies to the logical/sequential intelligence. Choice **c** is incorrect because it applies to the rhythmic intelligence.

**37. d.** When comparing or contrasting, the graphic organizer used is usually a Venn diagram. Choices **a**, **b**, and **c** are incorrect because the graphic organizer shown does not lend itself to those text structures.

**38. b.** This statement best pertains to a narrative. Choice **a** is incorrect because it describes journaling. Choice **c** is incorrect because it describes persuasive writing. Choice **d** is incorrect because it describes descriptive writing.

## Mathematics

**39. d.** The student did add, but he switched the values for the tens and ones place. Choice **a** is incorrect because he did use a zero as a placeholder for the hundreds place. Choice **b** is incorrect because he did add. Choice **c** is incorrect because he did use numerals.

**40. b.** Telling time is about angles of the clock hands. Choice **a** is incorrect because money and angles do not correlate. Choice **c** is incorrect because multiplication facts and angles do not correlate. Choice **d** is incorrect because patterns and angles do not correlate.

**41. c.** The order of operations (PEMDAS) states that one should do operations inside parentheses first, following the order of operations, which is $12 \times 3$. Choices **a** and **b** are incorrect because PEMDAS states that one should do all operations inside parentheses first, following the order of operations. Choice **d** is wrong because $12 \times 12$ would not be done in this problem.

**42. b.** She rounded to the nearest million rather than hundred thousand. Choice **a** is incorrect because she understood what rounding meant. Choice **c** is incorrect because the ten thousands place was irrelevant to her answer. Choice **d** is incorrect because she correctly rounded down but to the wrong place value.

**43. c.** The students must know that 12 inches equals 1 foot. Choice **a** is incorrect because an inch is not made up of feet. Choice **b** is incorrect because the size of an inch is only partial knowledge. Choice **d** is incorrect because it is irrelevant.

**44. b.** Skip counting is a form of multiplication. The number is being increased by nine: $63 + 9 = 72$. Choice **a** is wrong because the rules for dividing are not being used; the number is not being separated into parts. Choice **c** is incorrect because the numbers are not added together to make the next number. Choice **d** is incorrect because the numbers are not subtracted from one another to make the next number.

**45. c.** Changing the tens digit, 5, to 8 increases the value by 30. Choices **a**, **b**, and **d** are incorrect because if the number was changed to 83, the value would increase by 30.

**46. c.** The letter A has one vertical line of symmetry. B, C, and K have horizontal lines of symmetry.

**47. c.** Mrs. Howell is mostly likely basing her argument on the number of girls to boys and the probability of calling on one or the other. Choice **a** is incorrect because common sense is not the basis for a good argument. Choice **b** is incorrect because it would be challenging to find research that supports this reason for calling on more girls than boys. Choice **d** is incorrect because rational thinking has to do with actions following well-planned thoughts.

**48. b.** Distance, which is length, is measured. Choice **a** is incorrect because mass measures weight. Choice **c** is incorrect because capacity measures liquids. Choice **d** is incorrect because it is irrelevant.

**49. d.** The student did the correct operation, addition, but he didn't know that there are only 60 minutes in an hour. Choices **a** and **b** are incorrect because he did perform the correct operation, addition. Choice **c** is incorrect because we can't tell if he guessed.

**50. d.** Since the lumber is sold only in 6-foot lengths, he will have to buy 48 feet and have 5 feet left over. Choice **a** is incorrect because 42 feet are not enough. Choice **b** is incorrect because 43 is not a multiple of 6. Choice **c** is incorrect because it is not a multiple of 6.

**51. a.** Subtraction is the inverse operation of addition. Choices **b** and **c** are incorrect because they are not subtraction. Choice **d** is incorrect because although it is subtraction, it is not a correct calculation.

**52. b.** It should be $24.0 + 5.5 = 29.5$, not $24 + 5.5 = 7.9$. Choice **a** is incorrect because $24 - 5.5 = 18.5$. Choice **c** is only partially correct. Choice **d** is incorrect because $24 \div 5.5 = 4.36$ repeating.

**53. d.** The student calculated $28 \div 4 = 7$. Choice **a** is incorrect because the student multiplied $4 \times 28$. Choice **b** is incorrect because the student added $4 + 28$. Choice **c** is incorrect because the student subtracted $28 - 4$.

**54. d.** It would give him 9 bags. Choice **a** is incorrect because it would give him 60 bags. Choice **b** is incorrect because it would give him 48 bags. Choice **c** is incorrect because it would give him 324 bags.

**55. d.** The amount of supplies, 34, is divided by the number of days, 2. Choice **a** is incorrect because the number 16 has no value in this problem. Choice **b** is incorrect because the number 19 has no value in this problem. Choice **c** is incorrect because it is the wrong operation.

**56. a.** The teacher is using repetition to practice mastery of basic math facts. Choice **b** is incorrect because the teacher may use different lessons during each day. Choice **c** is incorrect because there are other ways of engaging students for afternoon learning. Choice **d** is incorrect because preparation for division would involve more than just drilling multiplication tables.

**57. a.** Students need to be taught how to find the least common multiple. Students are taught to multiply the denominators together, but that does not always give the least common denominator. Choice **b** is incorrect because fractions with different denominators cannot be added. Choice **c** is incorrect because the student would need to have found the least common denominator prior to multiplying it by the numerator and denominator. Choice **d** is incorrect because the identification of the numerator and denominator is taught during introduction of fractions; this is not an introductory question to fractions.

**58. b.** After the first digit of the dividend is divided by the divisor, students are to place the whole number above the division line on top of the first number and ignore any remainders. Choice **a** is incorrect because it states to divide the first digit of the divisor instead of the dividend. Choice **c** is incorrect because the step of bringing down the next digit of the dividend happens after choice **b**. Choice **d** is incorrect because students are taught to check their answer after the final step, when they have reached a conclusion.

**59. a.** The greatest common factor of two numbers, numerator and denominator, will allow students to find a number that goes into both numerator and denominator. Choice **b** is incorrect because multiples of 2 will not help students understand how to simplify fractions. Choice **c** is incorrect because students will need to divide after they have mastered the process of finding the greatest common factor of two numbers. Choice **d** is incorrect because vocabulary associated with fractions is taught as an introductory lesson; simplifying fractions is not an introductory lesson.

**60. a.** Without the place value, the number will be different. Choice **b** may be the result; however, the number value will ultimately be different, causing more confusion. Choice **c** is incorrect because the students can check their answers by using the reverse of division, which is multiplying. Choice **d** is incorrect because, while putting in a place value may help to keep the students' thoughts organized, it is more important that students get the right number value.

## Science

**61. a.** Students are being taught respect and responsibility by taking care of a living being. Choice **b** is incorrect because the concept of collaboration is not being demonstrated, and trust is a secondary objective. Choices **c** and **d** are incorrect because this assignment is not about the connections between living things, which would occur in their niche environment.

**62. c.** A diorama is a 3-D scene of an animal, object, or model in its natural setting or ecosystem. Choice **a** is incorrect because no mammal lives in outer space. Choice **b** is incorrect because it does not fulfill the requirements of a diorama. Choice **d** is incorrect because the assignment asks for only a single mammal.

**63. b.** The purpose of the scientific method is to create a universal system so that the same experiment can be repeated by looking at the original report. If the students make a mistake, they are then able to trace their steps back to find the mistake. Choice **a** is incorrect because the hypothesis may be proven incorrect. Choice **c** is incorrect because science is not 100 percent accurate; a better choice would be "a proven method for disproving outdated theories." Choice **d** is incorrect because one conducts an experiment to find a conclusion, not predict an outcome.

**64. d.** Students are given an unknown and asked to make an educated guess. Choice **a** is incorrect because students are taught to not guess, but to make *educated* guesses. Choice **b** is incorrect because students are not conducting an experiment. Choice **c** is incorrect because students are thinking analytically.

**65. c.** Physical science is the correct answer because the penny becomes clean through a chemical reaction. Choice **a** is incorrect because life science focuses on the characteristics of living things. Choice **b** is incorrect because earth science focuses on the physical features of the earth. Choice **d** is incorrect because health is not related to the chemical processes that would occur between soda and a penny.

**66. b.** Students are being taught how to classify butterflies based on the hierarchy of the taxonomic classification system. Choice **a** is incorrect because language and communication are not part of taxonomic classification. Choice **c** is incorrect because growth would fall under life processes, not taxonomy. Choice **d** is incorrect because there is no hypothesis to test.

**67. b.** An inverted triangle would feature the largest class and kingdom at the top and gradually narrow into specific species. Choices **a**, **c**, and **d** are incorrect because even though those graphs could be used to visually demonstrate this classification, they are not the best way to do so.

**68. b.** Cells are the building blocks of life because they are the base units of all organisms. Choice **a** is incorrect because cells are important. Choice **c** is incorrect because all organisms are composed of cells. Choice **d** is incorrect because cells can express different genes and have different physical characteristics.

**69. d.** Gas molecules move freely and have no definite volume or shape. Choice **a** is incorrect because gas does not have a definite volume or shape. Choice **b** is incorrect because gas does not have a definite volume. Choice **c** is incorrect because gas does not have a definite shape.

**70. b.** Solids have a definite shape and volume. Choice **a** is incorrect because not all solids are heavy. Choice **c** is incorrect because solids have a definite volume and cannot take the shape of the container they are placed in. Choice **d** is incorrect because the word *fluid* means something is liquid.

**71. a.** The law of conservation of energy states that energy cannot be destroyed. In the case of the car crash, the energy was transferred from the moving car to the parked car. Choice **b** is incorrect because the law of thermodynamics would not apply in this case. Choices **c** and **d** are incorrect because they are not actual laws of energy.

## Social Studies

**72. c.** The teacher is building cognitive effort in students by having the students think through and weigh all the possible options before arriving at a conclusion. Choice **a** is incorrect because there are more efficient ways to motivate students and maintain interest. Choice **b** is incorrect because flexibility is not a priority when the teacher is trying to stay on task. Choice **d** is incorrect because, while it is important to give students a voice, the central goal of the lesson is to determine the right answer to the question.

**73. c.** Cultural blending is the combining of cultures, and words from other places that have been adopted into the English language would give students a deeper understanding of cultural blending. Choice **a** is incorrect because researching the spread of democracy would focus too much on specific areas of the globe and not enough on cross-cultural exchange. Choice **b** is incorrect because the narrative of the *Mayflower* is an isolated event, and does not provide enough examples of cultural blending. Choice **d** is incorrect because economic topics are less relatable to fifth-grade students than language.

**74. b.** It is not valid to presuppose that the African American students will share the same perspective because they share the same ethnicity; students will come to historical events with a variety of perspectives. While it is not good to go into a lesson with presuppositions, choices **a**, **c**, and **d** are more feasible assumptions for a teacher to make.

**75. d.** Reciting from memory will allow for a deeper understanding of the words and meaning behind them. Students will also learn to put words together to express and communicate better. Choice **a** is incorrect because recitation is less about emphasizing different words than about committing whole works to memory. Choice **b** is incorrect because the goal of recitation is not to shorten the learning experience, but to allow students ample time to study and internalize texts. Choice **c** is incorrect because, in this case, the rhetorical or presentational techniques are secondary to the act of memorization.

**76. b.** The students would be required to investigate the government and possibly history and culture of colonial America to arrive at an answer. Choices **a** and **c** are incorrect because they focus more on the interpretation of texts rather than their historical context. Choice **d** is incorrect because it lacks a historical component.

**77. a.** A visual chart of the responsibilities of various levels of government would be the most efficient way of showing young students the relationship between community and state. Choice **b** is incorrect because authority figures alone do not show the relationship between community and state. Choice **c** is incorrect because the students will not learn about government by mere recitation. Choice **d** is incorrect because it is off topic.

**78. a.** It is a lesson regarding civic values. The students would learn of the issues debated by Federalists and anti-Federalists. Choice **b** is incorrect because it does not engage multiple opinions. Choice **c** is incorrect because it does not focus on how societies develop through civic competence; its focus is more on learning historical fact. Choice **d** is incorrect because it is too broad a topic.

**79. c.** The teacher should ask for more details that require students to piece together the story behind the picture to see how much they know about the time under study. Choice **a** is incorrect because it may not lead to further elaboration on the topic. Choice **b** is incorrect because, while this is an important point, it is more crucial for the students to provide further elaboration on the topic. Choice **d** is incorrect because it limits the discussion too early.

**80. b.** The lesson should activate students' ability to analyze the puzzle pieces and develop relationships. Choice **a** is incorrect because the puzzle pieces themselves do not have a qualitative component to judge. Choice **c** is incorrect because there is only a single solution for the puzzle. Choice **d** is incorrect because, while the lesson does activate perception, it is more targeted to analyzing relationships among the pieces.

**81. d.** The New Deal and Progressive reform movements fall under the category of government systems. Choice **a** is incorrect because, while both have elements of economic reform, they are not entirely based on economic principles. Choice **b** is incorrect because "human movement" is too generic a category. Choice **c** is incorrect because a proper comparing and contrasting of the two movements includes more than just their civic values.

**82. b.** Students have to comprehend material to make a prediction. Choice **a** is incorrect because students have to apply their knowledge to make a prediction. Choice **c** is incorrect because it is difficult to properly analyze a prediction, which is based on comprehension of facts. Choice **d** is incorrect because material is synthesized in the process of comprehension.

## Arts and Physical Education

**83. d.** A quarter note is a short note that is held for one beat and a rest, which is similar to the game red light, green light. Choices **a**, **b**, and **c** are incorrect because none of these games emphasizes the start-stop pattern of playing and holding quarter notes.

**84. d.** Rhythm is made when notes are combined into patterns. Choice **a** is incorrect because clapping for the pulse of a word demonstrates the opposite of extending a long note. Choice **b** is incorrect because clapping for the pulse of a word demonstrates the opposite of extending a measure. Choice **c** is incorrect because a symphony is a vast assemblage of instruments and sounds.

**85. b.** The teacher is checking for comprehension, or understanding. Choice **a** is incorrect because the students are being asked to apply learned knowledge. Choice **c** is incorrect because students are using prior knowledge. Choice **d** is incorrect because students are not being asked to analyze.

**86. a.** The teacher is instructing on still-life drawings. Choice **b** is incorrect because abstract art is nonrepresentational and still life is representational. Choice **c** is incorrect because a portrait drawing is a portrayal of a person. Choice **d** is incorrect because a collage is an assortment of materials or pictures.

**87. b.** Complementary colors like red and green produce white or black depending on whether they are colored lights or pigments. Choice **a** is incorrect because a primary color is any of a group of colors from which all other colors can be achieved by mixing. Choice **c** is incorrect because secondary colors are made as a result of mixing two primary colors. Choice **d** is incorrect because analogous colors are adjacent to each other on a color wheel.

**88. c.** Endurance is about being able to do a physical activity over a long period of time. Choices **a** and **b** are incorrect because these examples do not take place over a long period of time. Choice **d** is incorrect because recovery is about rest and regaining composure.

**89. b.** The body needs at least ten hours of sleep to revitalize itself. Choices **a** and **d** are incorrect, even though most people get only about seven to eight hours of sleep due to work schedules. Choice **c** is incorrect because this is almost depriving your body of rest.

**90. d.** Exercise is important for building strong muscles, improving overall health, and keeping weight down (choices **a**, **b**, and **c**).

**91. a.** Frequency refers to how often a person exercises. Choice **b** is incorrect because intensity refers to the amount of effort put forth in an exercise. Choice **c** is incorrect because time simply has to do with how many minutes or hours are spent exercising. Choice **d** is incorrect because it refers to the various kinds of exercises.

**92. d.** Type refers to the various kinds of exercises, such as cardiovascular or resistance training. Choice **a** is incorrect because frequency refers to how often a person exercises. Choice **b** is incorrect because intensity refers to the amount of effort put forth in an exercise. Choice **c** is incorrect because time simply has to do with how many minutes or hours are spent exercising.

**93. b.** Intensity refers to the amount of effort put forth in an exercise. Choice **a** is incorrect because frequency refers to how often a person exercises. Choice **c** is incorrect because time simply has to do with how many minutes or hours are spent exercising. Choice **d** is incorrect because it refers to the various kinds of exercises, such as cardiovascular or resistance training.

## General

**94. b.** The teacher should collect various forms of data to investigate questions about students' work, teacher practices, and learning. The data can help the teacher find strengths and weaknesses in both teaching and learning. Choice **a** is incorrect because it does not use the data to drive instructional decisions. Choice **c** is incorrect because a formative assessment will provide feedback on only one aspect of the lesson, while multiple aspects are required for improvements to teaching and learning. Choice **d** is incorrect because it would be effective only if the teacher reteaches the lesson.

**95. a.** An interdisciplinary lesson is one that incorporates the learning across various subjects. Choice **a** has students in a social studies class using science techniques to gain a deeper understanding. Choices **b**, **c**, and **d** do not incorporate other disciplines or subjects.

**96. a.** Students learning how to use information in a relevant manner through modeling and discussion is part of rigor, not relevance. Choices **b**, **c**, and **d** are all components of relevance.

**97. d.** Student-centered classrooms are the most effective learning environments. These classrooms allow students to learn through exploration, collaboration, and instructional guidance. Choice **a** is incorrect because teacher-centered classrooms are the least effective learning environments, as students do not fully engage in the learning. Choice **b** is incorrect because the parallel teaching method has two teachers covering the same material at the same time with different halves of the class. Choice **c** is incorrect because the station teaching method is a coteaching approach where students are divided into groups, thus slowing the efficiency of instruction.

**98. a.** It is important that teachers be familiar with teaching and learning because students learn best by actually doing. It is theorized that 90 percent of information is retained by what they do. Choice **b** is incorrect because it is theorized that only 20 percent is retained by what they hear. Choice **c** is incorrect because it is theorized that only 10 percent is retained by what they read. Choice **d** is incorrect because it is theorized that only 30 percent is retained by what they observe.

**99. d.** Learning centers, tiered lessons, and multiple intelligences are advantageous instructional methods that support diverse groups of learners. Choice **a** is incorrect because teachers are provided with a more detailed perspective of student learning through the collection of data. Choice **b** is incorrect because students should always be given an opportunity to work independently to deepen learning. Choice **c** is incorrect because the responsibility for learning should be shared by the student and teacher.

**100. d.** Tiered lessons allow for deeper instruction because each lesson is created with student readiness, learning style, and interest level in mind. Choices **a**, **b**, and **c** are reasons to tier a lesson.

**101. d.** Any time students can explore a primary source to get a better understanding, the learning is deeper. Choice **a** is incorrect because textbooks are secondary sources and usually left to the author's interpretation of an event. Choice **b** is incorrect, although it can be used as part of the research source; it just does not provide enough information. Choice **c** is incorrect because it would be an interpretation of the facts since a video of the actual time under study does not exist.

**102. b.** Teachers should treat students fairly by not treating them the same. Choice **a** is incorrect because the teacher should have communicated the difference between fair and equal with the class. Choice **c** is incorrect because children don't all need the same things. Choice **d** is incorrect because the understanding would be that everyone gets what they need and not everyone needs the same things.

**103. d.** Railroad tracks are the clearest example of parallel lines, because they do not intersect. Choice **a** is incorrect because intersections by definition are not parallel. Choices **b** and **c** are incorrect because both sidewalks and roads might intersect.

**104. b.** A group of four allows each child to have a job and give input. Choice **a** is incorrect because the group is too large and not everyone in the group will have a chance to share and be heard. Choice **c** is incorrect because someone will have to hold two jobs. Choice **d** is incorrect because the group is too large and not everyone is likely to be able to share ideas.

**105. c.** Authentic assessment does not look to isolate skills, but rather to examine a student's collective abilities. It emphasizes measuring what students know, not what they don't know (choice **a**), assesses collective abilities (choice **b**), and works to help students perform at higher levels of working and thinking (choice **d**).

**106. a.** Venn diagrams cannot display sequential order, which illustrates cause and effect. Choices **b**, **c**, and **d** are incorrect because Venn diagrams are well suited to showing common themes and comparing and contrasting information.

**107. c.** Students are encouraged to learn through discovery according to cognitive constructivist theory. Choice **a** is incorrect because it uses repertoires of passive and positive reinforcement. Choice **b** is incorrect because knowledge is acquired through social interactions. Choice **d** is not an educational theory.

**108. b.** Students' background knowledge is active during the review of previously learned material, so a connection can be made to what is to be learned. Choice **a** is incorrect because students are absorbing new material in this phase. Choice **c** is incorrect because students are being assisted while attempting the skill. Choice **d** is incorrect because students are applying the skill independent of the teacher.

**109. d.** Pretests are given for students to identify words that they can spell and to study the words that are unfamiliar. Choice **a** is incorrect because the students must learn the words before they can associate them. Choice **b** is incorrect because students should already know the rules for spelling prior to taking the pretest. Choice **c** is incorrect because students should already know how to sound out words prior to taking the pretest.

**110. a.** When students contribute to class rules, it is more likely they will buy in to following the rules. Choices **b** and **d** are incorrect because they will be by-products of buy-in to the rules. Choice **c** is incorrect because students may know a rule and not care to follow it.

## Note on Scoring

Your score on this multiple-choice exam is based on the number of questions you answered correctly; there is no guessing penalty for incorrect answers and no penalty for unanswered questions. The Educational Testing Service does not set passing scores for these tests, leaving this up to the institutions, state agencies, and associations that use the tests.

First find the total number of questions you got right on the entire test. As noted earlier, questions you skipped or got wrong don't count; just add up how many questions you got right.

Then, divide the number of questions you got right by the number of questions (110) to arrive at a percentage. You can check your score against the passing scores in the state or organization that requires you to take the exam.

If you are unsure of the passing score you will need, you can set yourself a goal of at least 70% of the answers right on each section of the exam. To find the percentage of questions you answered correctly, add up the number of correct answers and then divide by the total number of questions in each section to find your percentage.

What's just as important as your scores during this time of study is how you did on each of the sections tested by the exam. You need to diagnose your strengths and weaknesses so that you can concentrate your efforts as you prepare for the exam.

Use your percentage scores in conjunction with the LearningExpress Test Preparation guide in Chapter 2 of this book to help you devise a study plan. Then, turn to your study materials to work more on those sections that gave you the most trouble. You should plan to spend more time on the lessons that correspond to the questions you found hardest and less time on the lessons that correspond to areas in which you did well.

# 5 ▶ ELEMENTARY EDUCATION: CURRICULUM, INSTRUCTION, AND ASSESSMENT PRACTICE TEST 3

## CHAPTER SUMMARY

Here is the third full-length practice test for the Praxis II® Elementary Education: Curriculum, Instruction, and Assessment test. Now that you have taken two exams and brushed up on your studying, take this exam to see how much your score has improved.

Like Chapters 3 and 4, this chapter contains a full-length test that mirrors the Praxis II® Elementary Education: Curriculum, Instruction, and Assessment test. Though the actual exam you will take might be computer-based, the question types for each exam are replicated here for you in the book.

As you did for Practice Test 2, as you take this practice exam, you should simulate the actual test-taking experience as closely as you can. Find a quiet place to work where you won't be disturbed. Follow the time constraints noted at the beginning of the test.

After you finish taking your test, you should review the answer explanations. See the Note on Scoring after the last answer explanation to find information on how to score your exam.

Good luck!

| | | | | |
|---|---|---|---|---|
| 1. | ⓐ | ⓑ | ⓒ | ⓓ |
| 2. | ⓐ | ⓑ | ⓒ | ⓓ |
| 3. | ⓐ | ⓑ | ⓒ | ⓓ |
| 4. | ⓐ | ⓑ | ⓒ | ⓓ |
| 5. | ⓐ | ⓑ | ⓒ | ⓓ |
| 6. | ⓐ | ⓑ | ⓒ | ⓓ |
| 7. | ⓐ | ⓑ | ⓒ | ⓓ |
| 8. | ⓐ | ⓑ | ⓒ | ⓓ |
| 9. | ⓐ | ⓑ | ⓒ | ⓓ |
| 10. | ⓐ | ⓑ | ⓒ | ⓓ |
| 11. | ⓐ | ⓑ | ⓒ | ⓓ |
| 12. | ⓐ | ⓑ | ⓒ | ⓓ |
| 13. | ⓐ | ⓑ | ⓒ | ⓓ |
| 14. | ⓐ | ⓑ | ⓒ | ⓓ |
| 15. | ⓐ | ⓑ | ⓒ | ⓓ |
| 16. | ⓐ | ⓑ | ⓒ | ⓓ |
| 17. | ⓐ | ⓑ | ⓒ | ⓓ |
| 18. | ⓐ | ⓑ | ⓒ | ⓓ |
| 19. | ⓐ | ⓑ | ⓒ | ⓓ |
| 20. | ⓐ | ⓑ | ⓒ | ⓓ |
| 21. | ⓐ | ⓑ | ⓒ | ⓓ |
| 22. | ⓐ | ⓑ | ⓒ | ⓓ |
| 23. | ⓐ | ⓑ | ⓒ | ⓓ |
| 24. | ⓐ | ⓑ | ⓒ | ⓓ |
| 25. | ⓐ | ⓑ | ⓒ | ⓓ |
| 26. | ⓐ | ⓑ | ⓒ | ⓓ |
| 27. | ⓐ | ⓑ | ⓒ | ⓓ |
| 28. | ⓐ | ⓑ | ⓒ | ⓓ |
| 29. | ⓐ | ⓑ | ⓒ | ⓓ |
| 30. | ⓐ | ⓑ | ⓒ | ⓓ |
| 31. | ⓐ | ⓑ | ⓒ | ⓓ |
| 32. | ⓐ | ⓑ | ⓒ | ⓓ |
| 33. | ⓐ | ⓑ | ⓒ | ⓓ |
| 34. | ⓐ | ⓑ | ⓒ | ⓓ |
| 35. | ⓐ | ⓑ | ⓒ | ⓓ |
| 36. | ⓐ | ⓑ | ⓒ | ⓓ |
| 37. | ⓐ | ⓑ | ⓒ | ⓓ |

| | | | | |
|---|---|---|---|---|
| 38. | ⓐ | ⓑ | ⓒ | ⓓ |
| 39. | ⓐ | ⓑ | ⓒ | ⓓ |
| 40. | ⓐ | ⓑ | ⓒ | ⓓ |
| 41. | ⓐ | ⓑ | ⓒ | ⓓ |
| 42. | ⓐ | ⓑ | ⓒ | ⓓ |
| 43. | ⓐ | ⓑ | ⓒ | ⓓ |
| 44. | ⓐ | ⓑ | ⓒ | ⓓ |
| 45. | ⓐ | ⓑ | ⓒ | ⓓ |
| 46. | ⓐ | ⓑ | ⓒ | ⓓ |
| 47. | ⓐ | ⓑ | ⓒ | ⓓ |
| 48. | ⓐ | ⓑ | ⓒ | ⓓ |
| 49. | ⓐ | ⓑ | ⓒ | ⓓ |
| 50. | ⓐ | ⓑ | ⓒ | ⓓ |
| 51. | ⓐ | ⓑ | ⓒ | ⓓ |
| 52. | ⓐ | ⓑ | ⓒ | ⓓ |
| 53. | ⓐ | ⓑ | ⓒ | ⓓ |
| 54. | ⓐ | ⓑ | ⓒ | ⓓ |
| 55. | ⓐ | ⓑ | ⓒ | ⓓ |
| 56. | ⓐ | ⓑ | ⓒ | ⓓ |
| 57. | ⓐ | ⓑ | ⓒ | ⓓ |
| 58. | ⓐ | ⓑ | ⓒ | ⓓ |
| 59. | ⓐ | ⓑ | ⓒ | ⓓ |
| 60. | ⓐ | ⓑ | ⓒ | ⓓ |
| 61. | ⓐ | ⓑ | ⓒ | ⓓ |
| 62. | ⓐ | ⓑ | ⓒ | ⓓ |
| 63. | ⓐ | ⓑ | ⓒ | ⓓ |
| 64. | ⓐ | ⓑ | ⓒ | ⓓ |
| 65. | ⓐ | ⓑ | ⓒ | ⓓ |
| 66. | ⓐ | ⓑ | ⓒ | ⓓ |
| 67. | ⓐ | ⓑ | ⓒ | ⓓ |
| 68. | ⓐ | ⓑ | ⓒ | ⓓ |
| 69. | ⓐ | ⓑ | ⓒ | ⓓ |
| 70. | ⓐ | ⓑ | ⓒ | ⓓ |
| 71. | ⓐ | ⓑ | ⓒ | ⓓ |
| 72. | ⓐ | ⓑ | ⓒ | ⓓ |
| 73. | ⓐ | ⓑ | ⓒ | ⓓ |
| 74. | ⓐ | ⓑ | ⓒ | ⓓ |

| | | | | |
|---|---|---|---|---|
| 75. | ⓐ | ⓑ | ⓒ | ⓓ |
| 76. | ⓐ | ⓑ | ⓒ | ⓓ |
| 77. | ⓐ | ⓑ | ⓒ | ⓓ |
| 78. | ⓐ | ⓑ | ⓒ | ⓓ |
| 79. | ⓐ | ⓑ | ⓒ | ⓓ |
| 80. | ⓐ | ⓑ | ⓒ | ⓓ |
| 81. | ⓐ | ⓑ | ⓒ | ⓓ |
| 82. | ⓐ | ⓑ | ⓒ | ⓓ |
| 83. | ⓐ | ⓑ | ⓒ | ⓓ |
| 84. | ⓐ | ⓑ | ⓒ | ⓓ |
| 85. | ⓐ | ⓑ | ⓒ | ⓓ |
| 86. | ⓐ | ⓑ | ⓒ | ⓓ |
| 87. | ⓐ | ⓑ | ⓒ | ⓓ |
| 88. | ⓐ | ⓑ | ⓒ | ⓓ |
| 89. | ⓐ | ⓑ | ⓒ | ⓓ |
| 90. | ⓐ | ⓑ | ⓒ | ⓓ |
| 91. | ⓐ | ⓑ | ⓒ | ⓓ |
| 92. | ⓐ | ⓑ | ⓒ | ⓓ |
| 93. | ⓐ | ⓑ | ⓒ | ⓓ |
| 94. | ⓐ | ⓑ | ⓒ | ⓓ |
| 95. | ⓐ | ⓑ | ⓒ | ⓓ |
| 96. | ⓐ | ⓑ | ⓒ | ⓓ |
| 97. | ⓐ | ⓑ | ⓒ | ⓓ |
| 98. | ⓐ | ⓑ | ⓒ | ⓓ |
| 99. | ⓐ | ⓑ | ⓒ | ⓓ |
| 100. | ⓐ | ⓑ | ⓒ | ⓓ |
| 101. | ⓐ | ⓑ | ⓒ | ⓓ |
| 102. | ⓐ | ⓑ | ⓒ | ⓓ |
| 103. | ⓐ | ⓑ | ⓒ | ⓓ |
| 104. | ⓐ | ⓑ | ⓒ | ⓓ |
| 105. | ⓐ | ⓑ | ⓒ | ⓓ |
| 106. | ⓐ | ⓑ | ⓒ | ⓓ |
| 107. | ⓐ | ⓑ | ⓒ | ⓓ |
| 108. | ⓐ | ⓑ | ⓒ | ⓓ |
| 109. | ⓐ | ⓑ | ⓒ | ⓓ |
| 110. | ⓐ | ⓑ | ⓒ | ⓓ |

Time—120 minutes
110 Questions

**Directions:** Each of the questions or incomplete statements that follow is followed by four suggested answers or completions. Select the one that is best in each case and fill in the corresponding lettered space on the answer sheet with a heavy, dark mark so that you cannot see the letter.

# Reading and Language Arts

1. A parent asks her child's kindergarten teacher for advice on how to help the child with writing development at home. The teacher suggests keeping markers, pencils, and crayons available at home and helping the child write his name. What else should the teacher suggest?
   a. Allow the student to write text messages.
   b. Make sure that the student is not scribbling but writing letters.
   c. Involve the student with the parent's writing activities, like shopping lists and thank-you notes.
   d. Allow the child to watch videos on students writing.

2. What is differentiated instruction?
   a. process where a teacher changes the curriculum solely based on environmental preferences
   b. process where a teacher matches student characteristics to instruction and assessment with the same curriculum
   c. process where a teacher finds each student's learning style and bases activities on his or her needs
   d. process where a teacher determines a student's interest and creates a curriculum based on the student's interest only

3. A kindergarten teacher is planning a lesson where she is teaching letter-sound relationships in isolation, practice, and daily review, and allowing the students the opportunity to apply their knowledge of letter–sound relationships to the reading of phonetically spelled words that are familiar to them. What is the teacher teaching?
   a. orthography
   b. morphology
   c. letter sounds
   d. alphabetic principle

4. A new student from Haiti tells the teacher, "I hungry." The teacher recognizes that the student's native language lacks
   a. the morpheme *be*.
   b. the syntax *be*.
   c. the phonology *be*.
   d. the semantic *be*.

5. A prewriter holds up her work in class and proudly displays it. The teacher sees that the student wrote "mom iLFY." The child points to the words and translates the text as "Mom I love you." This child is able to do all of the following EXCEPT
   a. copy words from the room onto her paper.
   b. understand that print conveys meaning.
   c. demonstrate one-to-one correspondence.
   d. write "Mom" correctly, which is a frequently used word for this writer.

6. To help students with fluency, a teacher can use all of the following strategies in lesson planning EXCEPT
   a. shared reading.
   b. word walls.
   c. paired or partner reading.
   d. choral reading.

**7.** A teacher gives the class a graphic organizer to write an essay like the one below.

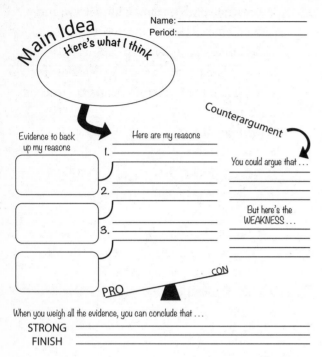

What type of writing does the teacher want the students to write?

**a.** narrative writing

**b.** descriptive writing

**c.** persuasive writing

**d.** journaling

**8.** A teacher gives students three words, *ship*, *mush*, *and flushed*, and asks them to identify the similar sound in the words. What is the teacher instructing the students?

**a.** phonemic awareness

**b.** spelling patterns

**c.** segmenting

**d.** phonics

**9.** A teacher has students playing a game where they are given a small number of picture cards. The teacher reads a word very, very slowly. The students have to look at the pictures and guess what word the teacher is saying, and then hold up the picture of the word they think the teacher is saying. What is the teacher instructing the students in?

**a.** onset and rime

**b.** syllabication

**c.** sight words

**d.** blending

**10.** A class is working in small groups during a writing lesson. They are focused on checking to make sure that they have all the elements of a story, looking for vocabulary words that they could use to make their writing more interesting, and finding where confusion is occurring in each other's writing. What part of the writing process are the students working on?

**a.** prewriting

**b.** revision

**c.** publishing

**d.** drafting

**11.** When a teacher is conducting an interactive read-aloud, he or she has to make sure to do all of the following EXCEPT

**a.** have students ask and answer questions.

**b.** have students make predictions.

**c.** use dramatic gestures and point to vocabulary words.

**d.** read the story once to the students.

**12.** If parents ask their child's teacher for some advice in helping the child learn outside of school, which of the following would NOT be sound advice?

**a.** Discuss current events at home.

**b.** Read with the child.

**c.** Use technology to help build the child's interest in reading.

**d.** Provide a tutor to help the child.

**13.** A teacher asks her second-grade students to discuss, in their triads, the different story elements in a short, realistic fiction passage and then present them to the class on a poster board. Which Common Core standard is she mostly addressing?

**a.** Follow agreed-upon rules for discussions (e.g., gaining the floor in respectful ways, listening to others with care, speaking one at a time about the topics and texts under discussion).

**b.** Ask and answer questions about what a speaker says in order to clarify comprehension, gather additional information, or deepen understanding of a topic or issue.

**c.** Create audio recordings of stories or poems; add drawings or other visual displays to stories or recountings of experiences when appropriate to clarify ideas, thoughts, and feelings.

**d.** Recount or describe key ideas or details from a text read aloud or information presented orally or through other media.

**14.** What is the primary purpose of guided reading?

**a.** to have students read and understand a text on their own

**b.** to have students understand new vocabulary words in a text

**c.** to have students learn how to use context clues

**d.** to have students understand letter–sound relationships

**15.** A teacher has one of the students in the class read out loud, and the teacher records mistakes and successes in the reading.

| page | E = errors  S-C = self-correction<br>M = meaning  S = structure  V = visual | E | S-C | E<br>M S V | S-C<br>M S V |
|---|---|---|---|---|---|
| 3 | ✓ ✓ ✓ of/sc ✓ ✓<br>The wheel comes off the truck. | | 1 | | M S ⓥ | M ⓢ V |
| 4 | ✓ ✓ ✓ ✓ ✓<br>It rolls down the hill.<br>✓ ✓ ✓<br>Faster and faster. | | | | |
| 5 | ✓ ✓ went/goes ✓ ✓ ✓<br>The wheel rolls through the field.<br>✓ ✓ p/✓ — ✓<br>It rolls past the cows.<br>✓R ✓ ✓<br>Faster and faster. | 1<br>1 | | ⓜⓢV | |
| 6 | ✓ ✓ ✓ ✓ ✓ farm<br>The wheel rolls through the barn.<br>✓ ✓ TA<br>It rolls [past the chickens.]<br>✓ ✓ ✓<br>Faster and faster. | 1<br>1 | | ⓜⓢV<br>M S V | |
| 7 | ✓ ✓ ✓ ✓Rz ✓ water<br>The wheel rolls toward the river.<br>✓ ✓ ✓ ✓ T<br>It rolls over the bridge.<br>✓ ✓ ✓<br>Faster and faster. | 1<br>1 | | ⓜⓢV<br>M S V | |
| 8 | ✓ ✓ ✓ in/sc ✓ ✓<br>The wheel rolls into the school.<br>✓ ✓ ✓ ✓ ✓<br>It rolls out of the door.<br>✓ ✓ ✓<br>Faster and faster.<br>✓ ✓ ✓ R ✓ ✓<br>The wheel rolls through the town. | 1 | 1 | M ⓢV | M S ⓥ |
| 9 | ✓ ✓ ✓ ✓ p/ ✓R<br>It rolls past the policeman.<br>✓ ✓<br>Faster and faster. | | | | |
| 10 | ✓ ✓ ✓ ✓ ✓ T<br>The wheel rolls into the garage.<br>✓ ✓ ✓<br>It stops rolling.<br>✓ ✓ ✓ ✓ ✓ track/sc<br>The wheel is on the truck. | 1 | 1 | M S V<br>M S ⓥ | ⓜⓢV |
| | **Totals** | 8 | 3 | | |

| Accuracy Rate: | 92% | Error Rate: | 1:12 | Self-Correction Rate: | 1:4 |
|---|---|---|---|---|---|

What is the teacher doing?

**a.** spelling test

**b.** informal reading inventory

**c.** nonsense-word fluency

**d.** running record

**16.** A school principal wants a teacher to bring in examples of formative assessments that he uses in class. What is one example that the teacher might bring in?

**a.** chapter tests

**b.** unit tests

**c.** student portfolios

**d.** students' reading response logs

**17.** A fifth-grade teacher wants to evaluate comprehension of a novel that was read within the class's literature circles. The teacher wants to use a summative assessment for the students. Which of the following should the teacher use?
  **a.** The teacher should require students to complete exit/admit slip.
  **b.** The teacher should record a discussion of the group.
  **c.** The teacher should have students write a book report about the novel.
  **d.** The teacher should require the students to complete a graphic organizer of the story structure.

**18.** All of the following are examples of how a teacher might perform a highly effective think-aloud EXCEPT
  **a.** selecting an enjoyable book or text.
  **b.** having students determine word meanings while the teacher is reading.
  **c.** modeling a reading strategy the students will be using.
  **d.** reading the book or text out loud while the teacher stops and shares what he or she is thinking.

**19.** In a fourth-grade classroom, there are various groups of students. Each group is reading a book based on their ability. The students are engaged in discussion about the text, with each of the students assigned a role within the group. The teacher is circling the room and making sure students are on task and answering questions when they arise. What activity are the students participating in?
  **a.** literature circles
  **b.** idea circles
  **c.** instruction conversations
  **d.** guided reading groups

**20.** What is shared writing?
  **a.** The students take a part of a story structure to create a unique writing piece when put together.
  **b.** The teacher and students work cooperatively together to compose a piece of writing.
  **c.** The teacher and students work on a writing piece with a partner.
  **d.** The students work together to present the teacher with a piece of writing.

**21.** The benefits of shared writing are all of the following EXCEPT that it
  **a.** reinforces and supports reading and writing.
  **b.** demonstrates the conventions of writing (e.g., spelling, punctuation, and grammar).
  **c.** allows all students to participate.
  **d.** allows students to decide on their writing topics.

**22.** At the end of a reading lesson, the teacher asks the students to write on a Post-it what they learned. As students exit the class to go to lunch, they stick their Post-its on a chart labeled "What Stuck with You?" What protocol is the teacher using?
  **a.** response log
  **b.** exit slips
  **c.** think, pair, share
  **d.** brainstorming

**23.** What is schema?
  **a.** background knowledge
  **b.** assessments
  **c.** teacher observations
  **d.** questions

**24.** A second-grade teacher asks students to tell her about snowflakes. The students then write on Post-its and stick them to a board with the title "Snowflakes." In subsequent lessons the teacher reads many nonfiction books about snowflakes and students add more Post-it notes to the board when they learn something new. What is the teacher creating with the students?
  **a.** bulletin board
  **b.** comprehension work
  **c.** graphic organizer
  **d.** schema chart

**25.** A teacher is teaching his first-grade class about poetry. The teacher asks the students to infer what a poet is thinking at the end of a poem. Which Common Core standard applies to answering this question?
  **a.** Read closely to determine what the text says explicitly and to make logical inferences from it; cite specific textual evidence when writing or speaking to support conclusions drawn from the text.
  **b.** Determine central ideas or themes of a text and analyze their development; summarize the key supporting details and ideas.
  **c.** Analyze how and why individuals, events, or ideas develop and interact over the course of a text.
  **d.** Interpret words and phrases as they are used in a text, including determining technical, connotative, and figurative meanings, and analyze how specific word choices shape meaning or tone.

**26.** A second grade teacher gives the following text to the class:

*Rabbit thought Turtle was slow, so he challenged Turtle to a race. But Rabbit was so confident that he would win the race he decided to take a nap during the race. Turtle knew he could win the race if he just kept on going. Turtle did just that and he WON!*

What literary genre does this text fall into?
  **a.** tall tale
  **b.** fable
  **c.** fairy tale
  **d.** folktale

**27.** A teacher asks her fifth-grade class several questions about their writing piece. The four questions are:

*1. Are the sentences grammatically correct?*
*2. Are the tenses in your writing consistent?*
*3. Are all sentences punctuated correctly?*
*4. Do all sentences start with a capital letter?*

What part of the writing process is the teacher going through with the students?
  **a.** prewriting
  **b.** drafting
  **c.** revising
  **d.** editing

**28.** A teacher has created a chart with the title "-og," and underneath it the words *dog, bog, log, fog, hog,* and *jog.* What strategy is being used with this anchor chart?
  **a.** morning message
  **b.** word building
  **c.** word families
  **d.** rhyming words

**29.** A teacher asks students to make a statement about the similarities and differences between characters in the novel *Number the Stars*. Which graphic organizer could the teacher use to teach this strategy?
a. sequence of events chart
b. Venn diagram
c. classification of information chart
d. details and main idea chart

**30.** A teacher gives students questions to answer while writing:

*Will you illustrate your writing?*
*Will you bind your work?*
*Will you read it out loud?*
*Will you display your writing in the room?*

What part of the writing process are the students in?
a. drafting
b. revising
c. editing
d. publishing

**31.** John is a student who is a struggling reader who knows only a few high-interest words. He does not have phonological awareness beyond whole word and syllable level. He can tap out syllables in familiar words. He enjoys listening to music and enjoys rap music. What strategies can the teacher use to help John improve his reading skills?
a. Assign him a text in line with his interests.
b. Have him print out and read the lyrics to his favorite rap song.
c. Partner him with a student with more advanced skills to read a text together.
d. all the above

**32.** A teacher reads a short fiction passage with the students and then asks them, "Which event or action occurred first?" What text element is the teacher teaching the students?
a. sequencing
b. main idea
c. making inferences
d. making predictions

**33.** All of the following are attributes of text that make it challenging for students, EXCEPT
a. lexical level.
b. sentence level.
c. text features.
d. discourse level.

**34.** According to Common Core state standards, teachers need to create text-dependent questions. Which of the following questions is an example of a text-dependent question?
a. What is it like to go to an open-air concert?
b. Who is Russell Freeman? How did he write this book?
c. Describe different types of concerts people go to.
d. Why had so many people come to the concert?

**35.** When a kindergartner is having trouble with spelling, the teacher can do all of the following EXCEPT
a. teach phonological awareness strategies.
b. teach high-interest words.
c. teach sound–letter relationships.
d. teach print and word concepts.

**36.** The following is an example of what level of phonological awareness?

*nap-kin*

a. word
b. syllable
c. onset-rime
d. phonemes

**37.** The following is an example of what level of phonological awareness?

*n-ap k-in*

a. word
b. syllable
c. onset-rime
d. phonemes

**38.** A teacher asks the students to tap out and count the syllables in words. What is the teacher assessing the students in?
a. word recognition
b. syllable recognition
c. onset-rime recognition
d. phoneme recognition

## Mathematics

**39.** A teacher asks a student to round the number 529,654. The student writes 529,700. What did the student do?
a. Round to the hundreds place
b. Round to the hundred-thousands place
c. Round to the nearest thousand, causing the digit in the ten-thousands place to change
d. Round to the ten-thousands place

**40.** A teacher says to her fourth-grade class, "James can invite only 22 families to his party. Some families have 3, 4, and 5 children. How many people can James expect at his party?" What level of Bloom's taxonomy is the teacher using?
a. synthesis
b. comprehension
c. knowledge
d. analysis

**41.** The teacher asks students to explain what form the number 44,004 is in. What should the students' response be?
a. ten thousands
b. word form
c. expanded form
d. standard form

**42.** Tamia has three crayons. Ariana has four times as many crayons. Write the equation that represents how many more crayons Ariana has than Tamia.
a. 34
b. $3 \times 4 = 12$
c. $4 - 3 = 1$
d. $3 + 4 = 7$

**43.** A teacher says to her fifth-grade class, "When you want to find the pattern, look at the first number and the second number. Then ask yourself, is it increasing or decreasing, and by how much?" What is the teacher having students do?
a. Solve in sequential order.
b. Solve using communicative property.
c. Create visual pictures.
d. Solve using associative property.

**44.** The teacher puts "Please **e**xcuse **m**y **d**ear **A**unt **S**ally" on the board for "parentheses, exponents, multiply, divide, add, subtract." What device is the teacher using to get the students to learn order of operations?
   **a.** mnemonic method
   **b.** association
   **c.** method of loci
   **d.** collaboration

**45.** The teacher asks students to read the number sentence $7 \times 3 = 21$ and identify the 7. What term defines the 7 in the sentence?
   **a.** product
   **b.** quotient
   **c.** factor
   **d.** addend

**46.** The teacher asks students to identify the property shown: $4 \times 5 = 5 \times 4$. What response does the teacher expect from students?
   **a.** commutative property
   **b.** associative property
   **c.** identity property
   **d.** zero property

**47.** The teacher wants third-grade students to know that they can arrive at the same value in different ways. If the students understand, which should they select as having the same value as $2 \times 7$?
   **a.** $2 + 7$
   **b.** $7 + 7$
   **c.** $7 + 7 + 7$
   **d.** $2 + 2 + 2$

**48.** What real-life shape should the teacher use to show students a hexagon?
   **a.**

   **b.**

   **c.**

   **d.**

**49.** Bill notices that he got a 63 on his test. When he questions his grade, the teacher tells him that the number in the tens place would be replaced by a 9. What will Bill's grade change to?
   **a.** 63
   **b.** 72
   **c.** 93
   **d.** 80

**50.** A second-grade teacher gives this problem: $32 + 7$; Max answers 102. What did he do wrong?
   **a.** He subtracted.
   **b.** He didn't line up the place values when he added.
   **c.** He added.
   **d.** He divided.

**51.** Jody's teacher puts in a jar the names of students who have completed all the homework for the week. The teacher wants to select from the jar the name of a student who will receive a free homework pass. There are 23 out of 31 names of students in the jar. What is the probability the teacher will choose Jody?
   **a.** 1 out of 31
   **b.** 22 out of 23
   **c.** 1 out of 23
   **d.** 23 out of 1

**52.** A second-grade teacher asks the class to estimate how long it would take to drive from the Grand Canyon to Yellowstone National Park. In what skill must the students be proficient to handle this task?
   **a.** units of measuring capacity and examples
   **b.** units of measuring distance and examples
   **c.** triangulation
   **d.** units of measuring weight and examples

**53.** A teacher puts a picture of a clock set at 4:00 P.M. on the board and asks students, "If I need to be at a meeting by 5:15 P.M. and it is 25 minutes away, what time should I leave by?" A student answers, "4:50." What did the student do to arrive at that answer?
   **a.** The student added the numbers together.
   **b.** The student subtracted the travel time from the start time of the meeting.
   **c.** The student added the time on the clock to the time of the meeting.
   **d.** The student subtracted the distance from the time school ends.

**54.** The teacher wants the students to fill in the missing cell. What should the students respond?

| Number of tables | 1 | 2 | 3 | 4 |
|---|---|---|---|---|
| Number of legs | 4 | 8 | ? | 16 |

   **a.** 12
   **b.** 20
   **c.** 7
   **d.** 9

**55.** A jogger ran 26,400 ft. in one day. How many miles did the jogger run?
   **a.** 5
   **b.** 31,680
   **c.** 21,120
   **d.** 5,280

**56.** A first-grade teacher asks students in her class to find the sum of 8 + 5 and then check their answers. What property should the students draw on to check their answers?
   **a.** inverse property
   **b.** identity property
   **c.** commutative property
   **d.** associative property

**57.** A fifth-grade teacher asks students to estimate the answer to this problem: 25.4 + 8.5. What values should the students add?
   **a.** 30 + 10
   **b.** 26 + 9
   **c.** 25 + 8
   **d.** 25 + 9

**58.** A fifth-grade teacher puts the following diagrams on the board and asks, "Based on the shading, which figure demonstrates perimeter?"

**a.**

**b.**

**c.**

**d.**

**59.** Ahsan has a total of 1,080 points on 12 tests. What expression can be used to find his test average?
   **a.** 1,080 + 12
   **b.** 1,080 − 12
   **c.** 1,080 × 12
   **d.** 1,080 ÷ 12

**60.** What is the fourth step in solving the equation $(30 - 5^2)^3 \div 25$?
   **a.** $5^2$
   **b.** 30 − 25
   **c.** $5^3$
   **d.** 125 ÷ 25

## Science

**61.** A fourth-grade science teacher is forming a lesson on meiosis. During meiosis, cells have half the number of chromosomes as body cells. This teacher decides to use fractions to illustrate the ideas. What instructional method is the teacher using?
   **a.** personal and social perspective of science
   **b.** creating connections between scientific disciplines and mathematics
   **c.** laboratory approach
   **d.** language and communication

**62.** A fourth-grade teacher lists the characteristics of mammals, including that mammals are endothermic and produce milk to nurse their young. Why does the teacher think it is important to list the characteristics of a broad group (like mammals)?
   **a.** to depict the similarities between other groups
   **b.** to create associations using characteristics that vary between organisms
   **c.** to identify the specialized functions of the group
   **d.** all of the above

**63.** The teacher has taken an ice cube out of the freezer and it turns to water. This change from a solid to a liquid is called *melting*. What type of change is the teacher depicting?
   **a.** chemical change
   **b.** physical change
   **c.** process of life
   **d.** condensation

**64.** The teacher presents two beakers to the class: one beaker has 200 ml of 70°F water, and the other has 200 ml of water that has been boiling on a hot plate. The teacher asks the students to predict what will happen when food coloring is added to both beakers. Student A says the food coloring will spread more quickly in the beaker with the boiling water. Student B says the food coloring will spread more quickly in the 70°F water. Which student is correct and why?
   **a.** Student A, because the molecules in the boiling water are moving slowly
   **b.** Student A, because the molecules in the boiling water are moving quickly
   **c.** Student B, because the molecules in the cool water are moving slowly
   **d.** Student B, because the molecules in the cool water are moving quickly

**65.** A teacher asks the class to find and classify rocks, shells, leaves, and seeds by shape and color. What form of instruction is being addressed?
   **a.** organization of scientific data
   **b.** science concepts and processes
   **c.** teaching methods
   **d.** scientific inquiry

**66.** The liquid that forms on the outside of a glass of ice water is called *condensation*. The teacher tells the students that condensation is created by a process similar to the formation of clouds. What form of technology could the teacher use to portray this point?
   **a.** telescope
   **b.** microscope
   **c.** computer simulation
   **d.** graphing calculator

**67.** Using the scientific method, after the students form a hypothesis, what should the teacher expect them to do next?
   **a.** Observe and record data.
   **b.** Identify a problem.
   **c.** Present their results.
   **d.** Conduct an experiment.

**68.** Fourth-grade students are learning how to use prefixes in science to better understand the classification of animals using scientific names. The teacher informs the students that there are two categories in an organism's scientific name. If the students understand the system, what term will they choose?
   **a.** trinominal
   **b.** tetranominal
   **c.** binominal
   **d.** uninominal

**69.** A teacher is teaching a lesson on converting temperature. The teacher wants the students to measure the weather in their town over a month to record on the class computer in order to predict weather patterns. What method of instruction is the teacher using?
   **a.** scientific inquiry
   **b.** model building and forecasting
   **c.** science concepts and processes
   **d.** problem solving

**70.** The teacher informs the class that heat, which is energy, is transferred from a hotter object to a cooler object. How could the teacher best demonstrate this process?
   **a.** by putting ice in boiling water
   **b.** by putting ice in cool water
   **c.** by placing an ice tray filled with (liquid) water in the freezer
   **d.** by placing an ice tray filled with ice back into the freezer

**71.** A fourth-grade teacher is describing the movement of heat through convection, which happens because a gas or liquid is heated and cooled. When heated, the gas or liquid rises, and then it falls when cooled because it is denser. The rise and fall create a convection current by which heat moves through gases and liquids. The teacher provides the information using what type of teaching method?
- **a.** guided discovery
- **b.** problem solving
- **c.** exposition and direct instruction
- **d.** situations and re-creations

## Social Studies

**72.** What is social studies content useful for?
- **a.** gathering relevant information
- **b.** distinguishing between fact and opinion
- **c.** presenting information
- **d.** determining word meaning

**73.** Which resource book would third-grade teachers make available to students when studying types of governments around the world?
- **a.** almanac
- **b.** atlas
- **c.** thesaurus
- **d.** dictionary

**74.** The teacher asks students to list nations that have the following kinds of governments: democracy, monarchy, and dictatorship. What level of thinking is being accessed?
- **a.** application
- **b.** knowledge
- **c.** evaluation
- **d.** synthesis

**75.** Vexillology is the study of flags. A nation's flag can give insight into understanding that country. Some teachers have students make replicas of flags from other countries to display in the class so that they can learn the significance of colors and symbols. How can the teacher ensure students will retain new knowledge over a long period of time?
- **a.** The teacher should test the students on the instructional objectives.
- **b.** The teacher should provide students with opportunities to practice with new knowledge.
- **c.** The teacher should instruct for a longer time.
- **d.** The teacher should integrate the lesson into another study.

**76.** The social studies teacher is having students read folktales and legends to learn about people around the world. What can NOT be learned from analyzing folktales and legends?
- **a.** values
- **b.** ideas
- **c.** beliefs
- **d.** empathy

**77.** The teacher asks which word means "the configuration of human behavior that includes ideas, beliefs, and values." What does the teacher expect the students to say?
- **a.** identity
- **b.** diversity
- **c.** empathy
- **d.** culture

**78.** The students are going to learn that people living in the western hemisphere have held differing assumptions about power, authority, ways of governing, and kinds of laws needed to encompass all the people of a nation. What subtopic would a lesson covering this material fall under?
a. environment and society
b. factors of production
c. interdependence
d. identity

**79.** The teacher is demonstrating to students how varying groups of people living in the western hemisphere may view the same issue or event differently. What is the teacher conveying to the students?
a. Change in attitude is good.
b. Empathy is gained by understanding the experience and thoughts of others.
c. Human systems are made up of unreliable information.
d. Government gives people choices.

**80.** The teacher has asked students to explain how a bill becomes a law. What instructional objective is being addressed?
a. Cite specific evidence to support analysis.
b. Determine the central ideas or information of a primary or secondary source.
c. Identify key steps in a text's description of a process.
d. Distinguish among fact, opinion, and judgment.

**81.** The teacher uses a flowchart to display information pertaining to events leading up to the American Revolution. What essential question would utilize students' understanding of analysis of the American Revolution?
a. What explanation do you have for the major causes of the American Revolution?
b. How would you describe the American Revolution?
c. How would you solve the overtaxation problem?
d. What is your opinion of the colonists' input toward the American Revolution?

**82.** The teacher asks students to write a research paper comparing the beginning of the twentieth century with that of the twenty-first century. Which instructional objective would be best for this task?
a. Cite specific textual evidence to support analysis of sources.
b. Determine the meaning of symbols and key terms.
c. Support claims with logical reasoning.
d. Develop a topic with relevant, well-chosen facts.

## Arts and Physical Education

**83.** The music teacher holds up the picture of this symbol.

What symbol is represented in the picture?
**a.** rest
**b.** treble clef
**c.** bass clef
**d.** half note

**84.** A student is reading a music sheet. He comes across a dotted quarter note in $\frac{4}{4}$ time. How long will he hold the note for?

**a.** one beat
**b.** $1\frac{1}{2}$ beats
**c.** $1\frac{1}{4}$ beats
**d.** $\frac{1}{8}$ beat

**85.** The teacher tells students that the time signature looks a lot like a fraction. The top number and the bottom number each have a purpose. The teacher asks, "In the time signature, what does the top number represent?" Which should the students reply?
**a.** the number of notes per minute
**b.** the type of note
**c.** what note receives one beat
**d.** the number of beats per measure

**86.** The teacher sets out samples of saturated fats that include cheese, butter, and cream, along with unsaturated fats that include vegetable oil. The teacher asks students to predict the state of each at room temperature. What should the students conclude?
**a.** solid; solid
**b.** liquid; liquid
**c.** solid; liquid
**d.** solid; gas

**87.** The teacher tells the students to gather important information about a particular food before eating it. It is important to determine how much energy a particular food will give you. What should the students look for to determine the energy the food will give?
**a.** number of calories
**b.** weight in grams
**c.** sodium percentage
**d.** amount of fat

**88.** The teacher displays a picture of the organ that stores a lot of the body's nutrients. Which organ does the teacher display for students?
**a.** stomach
**b.** liver
**c.** heart
**d.** brain

**89.** The teacher wants students to understand how important water is to the body. Which of these options describe(s) water?
**a.** Water is involved in all body processes.
**b.** Water makes up the basic part of the blood.
**c.** Water helps remove waste.
**d.** all of the above

**90.** The teacher wants to recommend a diet including carbohydrates that will break down more slowly. What type of carbohydrates should the teacher recommend to students?
a. simple
b. hard
c. complex
d. easy

**91.** The student wants to use green in the painting. Which primary colors will she need to mix?
a. yellow and blue
b. red and green
c. red and yellow
d. blue and red

**92.** The student wants to draw a shape with only one line of symmetry. Which shape should the student choose?
a. diamond
b. circle
c. heart
d. square

**93.** If a student chose two supplementary colors for the assignment, the two colors would be _____ each other on the color wheel.
a. across from
b. two colors away from
c. next to
d. none of the above

## General

**94.** A fifth-grade teacher has asked the social studies class to compare the statistical data from the 2008 and 2012 presidential elections. What level of higher-order thinking is this task?
a. knowledge
b. comprehension
c. application
d. synthesis

**95.** The students will be studying Abraham Lincoln's Gettysburg Address. Prior to reading, the teacher instructs the fifth-grade class on the events that led to the presidential address. What is the best reason for the teacher to provide background knowledge?
a. to distinguish facts and reasoned judgment
b. to determine the central idea or conclusions of the text
c. to aid in analysis of the author's purpose
d. to aid in citation of textual evidence to support analysis

**96.** Which part of Britain's government increased taxes in the American colonies to pay for the French and Indian War?
a. Parliament
b. proclamation
c. Townshend Act
d. Stamp Act

**97.** A fifth-grade teacher tells students data can be displayed in different ways. Which is the best way to display events over time?
a. $x$–$y$ plot
b. line graph
c. pie chart
d. bar graph

**98.** A third-grade class is learning about various cultures. While studying Latin American countries, the students learn to salsa and merengue. Which learning style is dominant in this lesson?
a. kinesthetic learning
b. role-playing
c. visual learning
d. auditory learning

**99.** What type of learning is the teacher catering to if she reads to her students aloud from a book?
a. kinesthetic learners
b. tactile learners
c. visual learners
d. auditory learners

**100.** A teacher develops a lesson plan that is tiered to meet the needs of students in an inclusive setting. The instructional objectives are clear and measurable. The teacher has included a way to get the students excited about learning by having them decipher a coded message. The lesson includes some hands-on activities, collaboration, and writing. What can be assumed?
a. The teacher has knowledge of a range of resources.
b. The teacher has the ability to design coherent instruction.
c. The teacher has established an environment of respect and rapport.
d. The teacher has established a culture for learning.

**101.** At the end of the lesson, the teacher realizes that only 17 out of 25 students thoroughly understood the instructional concept. What can be assumed?
a. The lesson was not entirely based on best practices.
b. The goals were probably not achievable and age appropriate.
c. There was very little use of authentic real-world assessments.
d. The teacher may not have appreciated each child's contribution.

**102.** A third-grade teacher voluntarily gathers data on reading performance and shares the findings of the research, including best practice techniques, to improve readability level of students with colleagues. What is the teacher demonstrating?
a. reflecting on teaching practice
b. demonstrating professionalism
c. professional growth and development
d. developing lessons based on best practice

**103.** The teachers are asked to be in constant contact with parents of students in class regarding student progress. What would be the best reason(s) for staying in contact with parents of students in class?
a. to establish a partnership with families
b. to keep parents informed about the instructional program
c. to build a sense of community
d. all of the above

**104.** The teacher asks students to read a story and use context clues. Which standard is being addressed by the teacher for use of context clues?
   **a.** Key ideas and details: Cite evidence to support analysis.
   **b.** Craft and structure: Determine meaning of words and phrases as they are used in the text.
   **c.** Integration of knowledge and ideas: Compare and contrast the experience of reading a story.
   **d.** Range of reading and level of text complexity: By end of year, students will read and comprehend literature.

**105.** The teacher asks students questions. Which question arouses higher-order thinking?
   **a.** What do you remember about the Battle of the Bulge?
   **b.** How would you differentiate between the Union and the Confederate armies?
   **c.** How could you develop the plot of the story?
   **d.** How can you describe the author's purpose?

**106.** To help create safe, secure, and productive learning environments, teachers can
   **a.** communicate clear and concise expectations to students and parents.
   **b.** instruct students on the guiding principles for conflict resolution.
   **c.** provide meaningful and prompt feedback.
   **d.** do all of the above

**107.** Which has the most significant influence on student learning?
   **a.** motivation
   **b.** classroom management
   **c.** differentiated lessons
   **d.** assessment techniques

**108.** What is the purpose of response to intervention (RtI)?
   **a.** to provide an environment for academic success
   **b.** to provide early concentrated strategies to interrupt student behavioral or academic difficulties
   **c.** to meet the needs of the individual students
   **d.** to describe student achievement and learning strengths and weaknesses

**109.** A teacher asks the second-grade class, "How many inches are there in two feet?" What is the teacher's purpose for this question?
   **a.** to assess prior knowledge
   **b.** to motivate students
   **c.** to differentiate instruction
   **d.** to see if the students know how many feet are in a yard

**110.** Anthony took ten tests, and the sum of his scores equaled 758 points. The teacher said the test average would be rounded to the nearest whole number. What is Anthony's test average?
   **a.** 75
   **b.** 75.8
   **c.** 76
   **d.** 80

# Answers and Explanations

## *Reading and Language Arts*

**1. c.** It is empowering to have a prewriter experience how writing is used in everyday life. Choice **a** is incorrect because a prewriter will not have the ability to write out messages at this point. Choice **b** is incorrect because at this stage in the student's ability it is important to allow him to scribble. Choice **d** is incorrect because it is important that the student experience writing with writing utensils.

**2. b.** All students should receive the same curriculum, but the teacher adapts activities and lessons based on ability. Choice **a** is incorrect because the teacher should not change a curriculum for each individual student. Choice **c** is incorrect because finding the students' learning styles is only one component of differentiated instruction. Choice **d** is incorrect because the teacher should not change the curriculum, but rather change activities so they are best suited to the student.

**3. d.** The alphabetic principle is the idea that letters and letter patterns represent the sounds of the spoken language. Choice **a** is incorrect because orthography is the teaching of spelling patterns. Choice **b** is incorrect because that pertains to the structural analysis of the language. Choice **c** is incorrect because the teacher is also teaching and reinforcing letter–sound relationships.

**4. a.** Morphology refers to the study of word formation, and many languages do not have the same tenses. Choice **b** is incorrect because syntax refers to the word order of the language. Choice **c** is incorrect because phonology refers to the sound system of the language. Choice **d** is incorrect because semantics refers to the study of meaning, words, and phrases.

**5. a.** The student might have copied the word "Mom" onto her paper, but the rest of the text was not properly copied. Choices **b**, **c**, and **d** all show what the student was able to do in her writing.

**6. b.** Word walls help students build vocabulary, not fluency. Choices **a**, **c**, and **d** do help with fluency.

**7. c.** The teacher is asking students to develop a logical argument and summary of the topic. Choice **a** is incorrect because narrative writing tells stories to express oneself. Choice **b** is incorrect because descriptive writing is describing a person, place, or thing to create a picture in the reader's mind. Choice **d** is incorrect because journaling allows students to generate ideas freely.

**8. a.** The teacher is asking the students to notice the sounds of the words. Choice **b** is incorrect because there is no spelling pattern in the words. Choice **c** is incorrect because students are not asked to segment the words. Choice **d** is incorrect because the teacher is not teaching phonics.

**9. d.** The game is teaching students to blend and identify words that are stretched out into basic sounds. Choice **a** is incorrect because the activity is not teaching onset and rime with the words. Choice **b** is incorrect because the activity does not ask students to find the number of syllables in each word. Choice **c** is incorrect because they are not asked to look at sight words.

**10. b.** The students are checking their drafts and making them better. Choice **a** is incorrect because prewriting involves getting lists and organizers before writing. Choice **c** is incorrect because publishing involves the finished product. Choice **d** is incorrect because drafting involves getting the story down on paper before checking the work.

**11. d.** It is important to read the text at least three times and reinforce vocabulary and questioning with the students. Choices **a**, **b**, and **c** are all strategies when doing an interactive read-aloud for students.

**12. d.** A teacher should give parents suggestions that will build conversation, reading, and questioning about the world around them. It is important to make time for conversation at home (choice **a**), reading with the child helps the child see that reading is important (choice **b**), and computers can help build interest in reading and provide help on words the child cannot read (choice **c**).

**13. d.** The teacher is asking the students to recall details from the story and to present them orally and visually. Choice **a** is incorrect because students are doing more than just discussing the question; the teacher is looking for students to do a specific activity. Choice **b** is incorrect because students are not asking questions about a speaker. Choice **c** is incorrect because the students are not asked to create audio recordings of stories or poems.

**14. a.** The main purpose of guided reading is to allow students to enjoy reading texts that are on their level while the teacher provides support for a small group. Choice **b** is incorrect because the main purpose of guided reading is not just to have students learn new vocabulary words. Choice **c** is incorrect because guided reading is not mainly about having students use context clues. Choice **d** is incorrect because students are encouraged to read with about 90 percent accuracy, and it is not just to help with letter–sound relationships.

**15. d.** A running record allows the teacher to assess the student's reading performance and the reader's behavior. Choice **a** is incorrect because the image does not show a spelling test. Choice **b** is incorrect because it does not show an informal reading inventory. Choice **c** is incorrect because the image does not show a nonsense-word fluency chart.

**16. d.** Formative assessments provide information for the teacher while learning is still happening; it quickly checks for student understanding. Choices **a**, **b**, and **c** are not correct because these are examples of summative assessments, which allow the teacher to evaluate student learning at the end of instructional units.

**17. c.** A book report will allow the teacher to evaluate student comprehension at the end of the novel. Choices **a**, **b**, and **d** are all examples of formative assessments that should allow the teacher to check for understanding throughout the lessons.

**18. b.** During a think-aloud the teacher is modeling everything he or she is thinking and students are observing. Choices **a**, **c**, and **d** are some examples of effective strategies for planning a think-aloud.

**19. a.** In literature circles students form groups to discuss a different text for each group. Choice **b** is incorrect because idea circles are groups of students who work together so that learning is focused on a concept learned in class. Choice **c** is incorrect because in instructional conversations the whole class is discussing a common text. Choice **d** is incorrect because in guided reading groups the teacher gives the students a prompt or big question that will guide them as they are reading.

**20. b.** When using shared writing in the class, the teacher is the scribe and both teacher and students work together to compose a writing piece. Choice **a** is incorrect because students are not working on their own to create a story. Choice **c** is incorrect because the teacher is the scribe in the process and reinforces certain concepts. Choice **d** is incorrect because the teacher is involved in student learning during shared writing.

**21. d.** In shared writing, the students do brainstorm together, but the purpose is not to have them choose a topic for writing. Choices **a**, **b**, and **c** are all benefits of shared writing.

**22. b.** At the end of a lesson, the teacher asks students to jot down what they learned and hand it in. This is an example of exit slips. Choice **a** is incorrect because response logs have students log in a notebook. Choice **c** is incorrect because think, pair, share is done during instruction and with a partner. Choice **d** is incorrect because the students are not brainstorming.

**23. a.** Schema refers to what a student knows and understands about a topic. Choices **b**, **c**, and **d** are incorrect because they are not examples of schema.

**24. d.** The teacher is asking about students' background knowledge and tapping into what they already know about a topic, which is represented in a schema chart. Choice **a** is incorrect because the teacher is evaluating students' prior knowledge of the topic. Choice **b** is incorrect because the students are not asked about comprehension of the books. Choice **c** is incorrect because the students are not asked to fill out a graphic organizer.

**25. a.** The teacher is asking students to infer what the poet might be feeling after the poem, so they need to support their thinking using evidence from the text. Choice **b** is incorrect because the question is not asking for a theme or to summarize the poem. Choice **c** is incorrect because it is not asking how a character, event, or idea develops in the poem. Choice **d** is incorrect because the question is not asking students to determine the meaning of words in the poem.

**26. b.** A fable is a narrative where the characters are talking animals and a moral is presented. Choice **a** is incorrect because a tall tale is exaggerated and is often about American frontiersmen. Choice **c** is incorrect because a fairy tale is usually about magical creatures and is geared toward children. Choice **d** is incorrect because a folktale is a legend that originated from oral tradition.

**27. d.** When students are asked to check for grammar, punctuation, and capitalization they are editing their writing. Choice **a** is incorrect because prewriting involves students brainstorming ideas about their writing choices. Choice **b** is incorrect because drafting involves students beginning to get their ideas down on paper. Choice **c** is incorrect because revision involves adding or removing elements from a writing piece.

**28. c.** The teacher is giving the students a group of words that have the same combinations of letters and sounds. Choice **a** is incorrect because the teacher is not giving the students the morning message. Choice **b** is incorrect because the students are not word building. Choice **d** is incorrect because the teacher is not teaching rhyming skills; the teacher is showing students the same combinations of letters and sounds.

**29. b.** A Venn diagram organizes the similarities and differences between two or more things. Choice **a** is incorrect because the teacher is not asking students to sequence events in the novel. Choice **c** is incorrect because the teacher is not classifying information in the novel. Choice **d** is incorrect because the teacher is not asking for main ideas and details in the novel.

**30. d.** When students are asked to think about displaying or sharing their work, they are at the publishing stage. Choice **a** is incorrect because when students are at the drafting stage they are starting to get their work on paper. Choice **b** is incorrect because when students are revising their work they are ensuring that it makes sense by taking out or adding more information. Choice **c** is incorrect because when students are in the editing stage they are correcting for grammar, punctuation, and spelling mistakes.

**31. d.** Choices **a**, **b**, and **c** are all valid means of helping the student improve his reading skills.

**32. a.** The teacher is asking the order in which things occurred in the story. Choice **b** is incorrect because the teacher is not asking about the big idea or gist of the story. Choices **c** and **d** are incorrect because the teacher is not asking what might happen next or what the information suggests.

**33. c.** The features in the text do not make it more challenging for students. Choices **a**, **b**, and **d** are all components that make it more difficult for students to understand a text.

**34. d.** Students have to analyze how a text makes connections among the ideas or events in the text. Choices **a**, **b**, and **c** are not text-dependent questions because they do not need the text to answer the questions.

**35. d.** The kindergarten student may not be ready to learn print and word concepts in order to understand spelling. Choices **a**, **b**, and **c** are all strategies that the teacher can use to help a kindergarten student with spelling.

**36. b.** The word is divided into syllables. Choice **a** is incorrect because the word would not be divided if this was the level of phonological awareness being recognized. Choice **c** is incorrect because the word would be further divided before the vowels to highlight onset and rime. Choice **d** is incorrect because the division of the word places emphasis on its syllables.

**37. c.** The example shows that the onset in the syllable is the consonant before the vowel, and the rime is the -*ap* and -*in* in the word. Choice **a** is incorrect because the word would not be divided if this was the level of phonological awareness being recognized. Choice **b** is incorrect because the word would not be divided multiple times if its syllables were being highlighted. Choice **d** is incorrect because the division of the word places emphasis on its onset and rime.

**38. b.** The teacher would be able to see whether the learners can hear and count syllables of words. Choice **a** is incorrect because the students are not asked to recognize words. Choice **c** is incorrect because the students are not asked to find the onset and rime in the word. Choice **d** is incorrect because the teacher is not asking the students to isolate each phoneme in each word.

## Mathematics

**39. a.** The student rounded to the hundreds place. Choice **b** is incorrect because the student's answer would be 500,000 if rounded to the nearest hundred-thousands place. Choice **c** is incorrect because the student's answer would be 530,000 if rounded to the nearest thousand, causing the digit in the ten-thousands place to change as well. Choice **d** is incorrect because the student's answer would be 530,000 if rounded to the ten-thousands place.

**40. a.** The students have to assemble the parts of the problem into the whole, making estimations about the families with multiple children. Choice **b** is incorrect because comprehension requires students to understand and interpret. Choice **c** is incorrect because to show knowledge, students only have to recognize information. Choice **d** is incorrect because analysis requires students to categorize information and show relationships.

**41. d.** The number is in standard form. Choice **a** is incorrect because it is irrelevant. Choice **b** is incorrect because the number is not written out. Choice **c** is incorrect because each place value is not expressed.

**42. b.** It is correct because $3 \times 4 = 12$. Choice **a** is incorrect because the numbers 3 and 4 were just put together. Choice **c** is incorrect because the numbers were subtracted. Choice **d** is incorrect because the numbers were added.

**43. c.** The teacher is asking student to do mental math and create a visual picture to solve the problem. Choice **a** is incorrect because the teacher is only asking students to use the first two numbers to start the pattern. Choices **b** and **d** are incorrect because these laws are not being used.

**44. a.** It is a mnemonic device to help students memorize steps in information. Choice **b** is incorrect because the words are not associated; they are substituted. Choice **c** is incorrect because the students are not visualizing information to recall it when needed. Choice **d** is incorrect because students are not working together.

**45. c.** Factors are multiplied to get a product. Choice **a** is incorrect because a product is the answer to a multiplication problem; 21 is the product. Choice **b** is incorrect because a quotient is the answer to a division problem; this is multiplication. Choice **d** is incorrect because addends are added; this is multiplication.

**46. a.** The commutative property means you can multiply numbers in any order. Choice **b** is incorrect because the associative property involves moving the groupings of parentheses, and there are no parentheses in this problem. Choice **c** is incorrect because the identity property is multiplying by 1; the students are not multiplying by 1 in this problem. Choice **d** is incorrect because the zero property is multiplying by zero; there is no zero in this problem.

**47. b.** It is correct because $7 + 7 = 14$ and $2 \times 7 = 14$. Choice **a** is incorrect because $2 + 7 = 9$ and $2 \times 7 = 14$. Choice **c** is incorrect because $7 + 7 + 7 = 21$ and $2 \times 7 = 14$. Choice **d** is incorrect because $2 + 2 + 2 = 6$ and $2 \times 7 = 14$.

**48. a.** A hexagon is a six-sided polygon. Choice **b** is wrong because the wedge is a three-sided polygon, a triangle. Choice **c** is wrong because this is an eight-sided polygon, an octagon. Choice **d** is wrong because this is a four-sided polygon, a quadrilateral.

**49. c.** Changing the tens digit, 6, to 9 changes the value to 93. Choice **a** is incorrect because there was no change. Choice **b** is incorrect because if it were changed to 72, the ones place would have been increased by 9. Choice **d** is incorrect because there was an increase of 17.

**50. b.** He did not correctly line up the place values. It should be $32 + 7 = 39$. Choice **a** is incorrect because $32 - 7 = 25$. Choice **c** is only partially correct and does not explain how Max arrived at the wrong answer. Choice **d** is incorrect because $32 \div 7 = 4.6$.

**51. c.** One name of one student out of the jar of 23 names will be chosen. Choice **a** is incorrect because the jar does not contain the names of all 31 children in the class. Choice **b** is incorrect because only one student will be selected for the free homework pass, not 22. Choice **d** is incorrect because the numbers are reversed.

**52. b.** Distance, which is length, would need to be applied to this example. Choice **a** is incorrect because capacity measures the amount something can contain. Choice **c** is incorrect because it is irrelevant. Choice **d** is incorrect because weight measures the gravitational pull on an object.

**53. b.** The student subtracted the travel time of 25 minutes from the start time of 5:15 P.M. to get 4:50. Choice **a** is incorrect because the student would have concluded 5:40. Choice **c** is incorrect because the student would have concluded 9:15. Choice **d** is incorrect because the time school ends is irrelevant to the problem.

**54. a.** The rule is to multiply the number of tables times 4; $3 \times 4 = 12$. Choice **b** is incorrect because $3 \times 4 = 12$, not 20. Choice **c** is incorrect because $3 \times 4 = 12$, and this is $3 + 4 = 7$. Choice **d** is incorrect because $3 \times 4 = 12$, and this is $3 \times 3 = 9$.

**55. a.** 26,400 divided by 5,280 equals 5 miles. Choice **b** is incorrect because the incorrect operation was performed; the number of feet run and the number of feet in a mile were added. Choice **c** is an incorrect operation because the numbers were subtracted. Choice **d** is incorrect because it is the number of feet in a mile; the computation was not completed.

**56. a.** The inverse property is the way to check that the answer is correct. By taking the sum, 13, and subtracting either 8 or 5 from it, the result will be 5 or 8, indicating that the numbers have been added correctly. Choice **b** is incorrect because it refers to the fact that the sum of a number and zero is the number itself. Choice **c** is incorrect because it means you can add numbers in any order. Choice **d** is incorrect because grouping is not involved.

**57. d.** The numbers get rounded to the same place value. Choice **a** is incorrect because the numbers have been rounded too high. Choice **b** is incorrect because only one of the numbers has been rounded correctly. Choice **c** is incorrect because only one of the numbers has been rounded correctly.

**58. d.** Perimeter is the distance around a figure, so just the outline of the shape should be shaded. The other choices are incorrect because they show area.

**59. d.** Dividing the total number of points, 1,080, by the number of tests, 12, would yield the average, 90. Choice **a** is incorrect because it is addition. Choice **b** is incorrect because it is subtraction. Choice **c** is incorrect because it is multiplication.

**60. d.** Using PEMDAS, the fourth step is dividing. Choice **a** is incorrect because it shows the first step of PEMDAS. Choice **b** is incorrect because it is the second step. Choice **c** is incorrect because it is the third step.

## Science

**61. b.** A fraction is used in mathematics and is a numerical quantity that is not a whole number. When a teacher asks the students to use fractions to describe scientific processes, they are creating connections between science and mathematics. Choice **a** is incorrect because the data used is neither personal nor social in nature. Choice **c** is incorrect because the use of fractions is a cross-curricular approach that is not confined to the laboratory. Choice **d** is incorrect because the use of fractions is mathematical, not based in language and communication.

**62. c.** When listing the characteristics of a group, you are identifying the specialized functions and creating associations using similar characteristics that differ when compared to other groups. Choice **a** is incorrect because the characteristics listed stay within the mammal group. Choice **b** is incorrect because the characteristics listed focus on shared traits, not varying traits. Choice **d** is incorrect because choices **a** and **b** are incorrect.

**63. b.** The change from solid ice to liquid water is a physical change. Choice **a** is incorrect because a chemical change would be a change that results in a new substance. Choice **c** is incorrect because water is not a living organism, and thus the change cannot be considered a process of life. Choice **d** is incorrect because condensation is the conversion of a vapor or gas to a liquid.

**64. b.** As the temperature rises, the molecules move more quickly toward chaos. The food coloring will spread more quickly in the boiling water with the faster-moving molecules. Choice **a** is incorrect because the boiling water increases the speed of the moving molecules. Choice **c** is incorrect because the food coloring will spread more quickly in the boiling water with the faster-moving molecules. Choice **d** is incorrect because the molecules in the cool water move more slowly than those in the boiling water.

**65. a.** The classification of organisms and materials falls into the category of organization of scientific data. Choice **b** is incorrect because the process of classification alone does not address science concepts and processes. Choice **c** is incorrect because the process of classification does not address teaching methods. Choice **d** is incorrect because there would need to be something being tested to address scientific inquiry.

**66. c.** A computer simulation could take the class through various systems of condensation. Choices **a**, **b**, and **d** are incorrect because a telescope, microscope, and graphing calculator would not be effective mediums to observe condensation.

**67. d.** The steps to the scientific method go as follows: identify a problem, form a hypothesis, conduct an experiment, observe and record data, and finally determine results and conclusion. Choices **a**, **b**, and **c** are incorrect because they do not follow the formation of a hypothesis in the order of the scientific method.

**68. c.** If the students understand the listed prefixes, *tri-* (three), *tetra-* (four), *bi-* (two), and *uni-* (one), the appropriate choice would be *binominal*. Choices **a**, **b**, and **d** are incorrect because the prefixes do not align with the concept of *two* categories in an organism's scientific name.

**69. b.** This assignment would fall under model building and forecasting because it consists of the use of plans and computer simulations. Choice **a** is incorrect because scientific inquiry consists of solving problems, constructing explanations, and communicating results. Choice **c** is incorrect because this activity would not fall into the area of science concepts and processes. Choice **d** is incorrect because the assignment more specifically targets model building and forecasting as part of an overall problem-solving process.

**70. a.** When ice is put in boiling water, the heat from the boiling water will be transferred to the colder ice cubes and melt them. Choices **b**, **c**, and **d** are incorrect because none of the examples will result in an immediately discernible change.

**71. c.** The teacher guides the students through the mentioned process using exposition and direct instruction. Choices **a**, **b**, and **d** are incorrect because there is no discovery, problem, or situation for the students to solve or re-create, because all the information is presented to them.

## Social Studies

**72. b.** The area of social studies is filled with facts, events, and records to distinguish between fact and opinion. Choice **a** is incorrect because it is relevant to writing. Choice **c** is incorrect because it is relevant to expressing information. Choice **d** is incorrect because it is relevant to conventions of English.

**73. a.** An almanac is a reference of current information. Choice **b** is incorrect because an atlas is made up primarily of maps used to locate places. Choice **c** is incorrect because a thesaurus is a book of synonyms and antonyms. Choice **d** is incorrect because a dictionary is a book of definitions.

**74. b.** Listing is the lowest level of cognition. Choice **a** is incorrect because the student is not being asked to apply knowledge. Choice **c** is incorrect because the student is not being asked to make an informed judgment. Choice **d** is incorrect because the student is not combining concepts.

**75. b.** Students must be able to use new knowledge if they are to retain it. Choice **a** is incorrect because instructional objectives are not being discussed. Choice **c** is incorrect because unless students practice using information, it does not matter how long the teacher instructs. Choice **d** is incorrect because this only exposes students to the lesson over and over.

**76. d.** The students cannot learn to be empathetic from this lesson, because they may not be able to identify similar experiences, behaviors, and responses. However, students can learn choices **a**, **b**, and **c** from this lesson.

**77. d.** Culture is a way of life that includes patterns of behavior, ideas, values, and beliefs. Choice **a** is incorrect because identity is an awareness of one's values and beliefs as an individual and member of a group. Choice **b** is incorrect because diversity relates to understanding and respecting others' differences and similarities. Choice **c** is incorrect because being empathetic means being able to internalize the experience of others.

**78. d.** Identity is an awareness of one's values and beliefs as an individual and member of a group. Choice **a** is incorrect because it has to do with geography and how human activity is influenced. Choice **b** is incorrect because it has to do with the resources of a place (human resources included). Choice **c** is incorrect because it has to do with relying on others in a fair exchange.

**79. b.** The teacher is trying to connect students to learning through empathy. Being empathetic means being able to internalize the experience of others. Choice **a** is incorrect because it is an expression that doesn't connect to the lesson. Choice **c** is incorrect because it is a false statement. Choice **d** is incorrect because it has no relevance to the topic.

**80. c.** The teacher wants students to explain the process. Choice **a** is incorrect because it does not include the explanation of the process. Choice **b** is incorrect because the central theme is not being asked to be identified. Choice **d** is incorrect because it does not connect to the task.

**81. a.** The students will have to show relationships between major causes. Choice **b** is incorrect because it only requires students to recall or recognize information. Choice **c** is incorrect because it is at the application level; students have to apply their knowledge. Choice **d** is incorrect because it would have students make judgments, which are at the evaluation level.

**82. d.** The teacher would want students to be able to develop a topic and collect relevant facts from the broad task. Choice **a** is incorrect because the students are not doing an analysis. Choice **b** is incorrect because they are not looking at historical facts symbolically. Choice **c** is incorrect because it is implied in choice **d** that the students will be able to support their claims.

## Arts and Physical Education

**83. b.** The picture is an image of a treble clef. Choices **a**, **c**, and **d** are incorrect.

**84. b.** A dotted quarter note ($\downarrow$.) is held for $1\frac{1}{2}$ beats. Choices **a**, **c**, and **d** are incorrect.

**85. d.** The top number in the time signature represents the number of beats per measure. Choices **a** and **b** are incorrect because they have no relation to the time signature. Choice **c** is incorrect because that is what the bottom number in a time signature would represent.

**86. c.** Saturated fats are usually solid at room temperature and unhealthier than unsaturated fats. Unsaturated fats are usually liquid at room temperature and necessary for the body in small amounts. Choices **a**, **b**, and **d** are incorrect.

**87. a.** The number of calories in a food lets you know how much energy the food will give you. Choices **b**, **c**, and **d** are incorrect because they tell the amount in grams, amount of salt present, and the amount of fat present, respectively.

**88. b.** The liver is the storage place for most of the body's nutrients. Choice **a** is incorrect because the stomach is the location where food starts to be broken down, not stored. Choices **c** and **d** are incorrect because they are not involved in the digestive tract.

**89. d.** Water is involved in all of the body's processes. It makes up the basic part of the blood, removes waste, and regulates body temperature.

**90. c.** Complex carbohydrates break down more slowly than simple carbohydrates (choice **a**). Choices **b** and **d** are incorrect because they are not types of carbohydrates.

**91. a.** By mixing blue and yellow, you can produce green. Choice **b** is incorrect because green is not a primary color. Choices **c** and **d** are incorrect because they would produce orange or purple, respectively.

**92. c.** A heart would have only one line of symmetry, whereas choices **a**, **b**, and **d** have two or more.

**93. c.** Supplementary colors are next to each other on the color wheel. Choice **a** is incorrect because complementary colors are across from each other. Choice **b** is incorrect because there is no name for the color two colors away on the color wheel.

## General

**94. c.** According to Bloom's taxonomy, to compare is to apply skills and knowledge in other situations. Choice **a** is incorrect because it is just the recall of facts. Choice **b** is incorrect because it is the process of understanding knowledge. Choice **d** is incorrect because synthesis is higher-order thinking allowing students to take parts and create a whole.

**95. c.** The teacher is looking to provide students with the full scope and sequence of what led up to the Gettysburg Address. Choice **a** is incorrect because the students will not be distinguishing facts and reasoned judgment. Choice **b** is incorrect because students should be able to determine the central idea or conclusions of the text without background knowledge. Choice **d** is incorrect because evidence can be cited to support analysis without background knowledge.

**96. a.** Parliament, Britain's lawmaking body, increased taxes. Choice **b** is incorrect because a proclamation is an official announcement made by a government. Choice **c** is incorrect because the Townshend Act taxed goods brought into the colonies from Britain. Choice **d** is incorrect because the Stamp Act put a tax on documents. Choices **b**, **c**, and **d** are not parts of government.

**97. b.** Using a line graph is the best way for students to display events over time. Line graphs show chronology. Choice **a** is incorrect because *x–y* plots show relationships between two or more data. Choice **c** is incorrect because pie charts are best used to represent parts of a whole. Choice **d** is incorrect because bar graphs are used to compare data between two or more items.

**98. a.** Kinesthetic learning is correct, because it is active hands-on experience. Choice **b** is incorrect because role-playing is not a learning style. Choice **c** is incorrect because visual lessons have more to do with observing. Choice **d** is incorrect because auditory learning has more to do with listening.

**99. d.** Auditory learners would rather listen to things than read about them. Choice **a** is incorrect because kinesthetic learners learn best from hands-on experience. Choice **b** is incorrect because tactile learners, like kinesthetic learners, learn best from experience or doing. Choice **c** is incorrect because visual learners learn best by seeing something done.

**100. b.** The teacher is demonstrating an ability to design coherent instruction that centers on the needs of the students. Choice **a** is incorrect because knowledge of a range of resources includes things such as texts, instructional aids, field trips, and technology. Choice **c** is incorrect because an environment of respect and rapport has to do with establishing relationships with students that allow the students to flourish. Such measures could include showing appreciation, providing opportunities to get to know one another, and encouraging students to take risks. Choice **d** is incorrect because an established culture for learning has to do with setup of the classroom, display of student work, and evidence of feedback to students.

**101. a.** The best way to demonstrate knowledge of subject and pedagogy is to develop lessons based fully on best practices. Choice **b** is incorrect because goals are developed along with instructional outcomes. Choice **c** is incorrect because assessments are ways of obtaining useful feedback. Choice **d** is incorrect because demonstrating an appreciation for each individual student lends itself to creating an environment of respect and rapport.

**102. c.** The teacher is demonstrating professional growth and development by taking the initiative to gather research data and share findings with best practice techniques with colleagues. Choice **a** is incorrect because reflection has to do with thinking about parts of a lesson to see what went right and what needs improvement. Choice **b** is incorrect because professionalism has more to do with demonstrating integrity and ethical conduct through interactions with students and colleagues. Choice **d** is incorrect because it demonstrates knowledge of subject and pedagogy based on best practices.

**103. d.** There are many reasons to make contact with parents of students in the class. The best reasons are to establish a partnership with families (choice **a**), keep parents informed about the instructional program (choice **b**), and build a sense of community (choice **c**). All of these actions support student learning.

**104. b.** The reading standard that incorporates the use of context clues falls under craft and structure. The other choices do not have to do with context clues.

**105. c.** This question allows students to use and apply their ideas, theories, and problem-solving techniques in a new way. Choice **a** is incorrect because it asks students to recall information which is at the lowest level. Choice **b** is incorrect because students can answer in their own words by stating facts, which is at level 2 (comprehension). Choice **d** is incorrect because it asks students to recall and present information, which is at level 1.

**106. d.** Teachers need to promote an atmosphere that fosters learning. In order to do that, the teacher needs to communicate clear and concise expectations to students and parents (choice **a**), instruct students on the guiding principles for conflict resolution (choice **b**), and provide meaningful and prompt feedback (choice **c**).

**107. a.** Motivation has the most significant influence. However, classroom management (choice **b**) is important as it helps to provide an environment conducive to academic success. Differentiated lessons (choice **c**) are tailored to meet the needs of the individual students. Assessment strategies (choice **d**) are used to describe student achievement and learning strengths and weaknesses.

**108. b.** RtI is a framework for early concentrated intervention that centers on individual student difficulties. Choice **a** is incorrect because it has more to do with motivation. Choice **c** is incorrect because it has more to do with differentiated instruction. Choice **d** is incorrect because it has more to do with assessment techniques.

**109. a.** The teacher is trying to assess how much the students know prior to starting the lesson. Choice **b** is incorrect because the teacher is asking students to recall information learned rather than trying to motivate them. Choice **c** is incorrect because the teacher is not meeting the individual needs of the students. Choice **d** is incorrect because it is irrelevant.

**110. c.** The average is calculated by 758 divided by 10, which equals 75.8. Because 8 is greater than 5, the number is rounded up to 76. Choice **a** is incorrect because the points were rounded down. Choice **b** is incorrect because the number was not rounded to the nearest whole number. Choice **d** is incorrect because it was rounded to nearest tens place.

## Note on Scoring

Your score on this multiple-choice exam is based on the number of questions you answered correctly; there is no guessing penalty for incorrect answers and no penalty for unanswered questions. The Educational Testing Service does not set passing scores for these tests, leaving this up to the institutions, state agencies, and associations that use the tests.

First find the total number of questions you got right on the entire test. As noted earlier, questions you skipped or got wrong don't count; just add up how many questions you got right.

Then, divide the number of questions you got right by the number of questions (110) to arrive at a percentage. You can check your score against the passing scores in the state or organization that requires you to take the exam.

If you are unsure of the passing score you will need, you can set yourself a goal of at least 70% of the answers right on each section of the exam. To find the percentage of questions you answered correctly, add up the number of correct answers and then divide by the total number of questions in each section to find your percentage.

What's just as important as your scores during this time of study is how you did on each of the sections tested by the exam. You need to diagnose your strengths and weaknesses so that you can concentrate your efforts as you prepare for the exam.

Use your percentage scores in conjunction with the LearningExpress Test Preparation guide in Chapter 2 of this book to help you devise a study plan. Then, turn to your study materials to work more on those sections that gave you the most trouble. You should plan to spend more time on the lessons that correspond to the questions you found hardest and less time on the lessons that correspond to areas in which you did well.

# ADDITIONAL ONLINE PRACTICE

Using the codes below, you'll be able to log in and access additional online practice materials!

**Your free online practice access code is:**
**FVEN6VS6151FUAC5FJVL**

Follow these simple steps to redeem your code:

- Go to **www.learningexpresshub.com/affiliate** and have your access code handy.

**If you're a new user:**
- Click the **New user? Register here** button and complete the registration form to create your account and access your products.
- Be sure to enter your unique access code only once. If you have multiple access codes, you can enter them all—just use a comma to separate each code.
- The next time you visit, simply click the **Returning user? Sign in** button and enter your username and password.
- Do not re-enter previously redeemed access code. Any products you previously accessed are saved in the **My Account** section on the site. Entering a previously redeemed access code will result in an error message.

**If you're a returning user:**
- Click the **Returning user? Sign in** button, enter your username and password, and click **Sign In**.
- You will automatically be brought to the **My Account** page to access your products.
- Do not re-enter previously redeemed access code. Any products you previously accessed are saved in the **My Account** section on the site. Entering a previously redeemed access code will result in an error message.

**If you're a returning user with a new access code:**
- Click the **Returning user? Sign in** button, enter your username, password, and new access code, and click **Sign In**.
- If you have multiple access codes, you can enter them all—just use a comma to separate each code.
- Do not re-enter previously redeemed access code. Any products you previously accessed are saved in the **My Account** section on the site. Entering a previously redeemed access code will result in an error message.

If you have any questions, please contact LearningExpress Customer Support at LXHub@LearningExpressHub .com. All inquiries will be responded to within a 24-hour period during our normal business hours: 9:00 A.M.– 5:00 P.M. Eastern Time. Thank you!

# NOTES

# NOTES

NOTES

# NOTES